MY VIETNAM JOURNEY

TOLD IN 50 SHORT STORIES

This is written for my wife Janet, my children
Lynda, Philip, and Elizabeth, their spouses and offspring.

There are many myths that get created over time;
these stories best present facts as they occurred.

Also by Donald C. Strauss

Customize…don't minimize…Your Retirement
7 Paths to Explore, Possibilities, Choices,
and Your Future Happiness

Acknowledgements

It has taken several years to write this book and many wondered if it would ever be completed. To all who expressed surprise about this work, but encouragement to see it through, I say, "Thank You!"

Thanks go out to Janet Rand and Lynn Shereshewsky, two long time friends, who took the time to read this manuscript and who encouraged me to publish this work. I appreciate the fact that both believed this book had universal appeal that should be available beyond just a few friends and relatives.

A special thank you also goes to my wife, Jan, who found old photographs and other materials to be inserted to support the written word.

Finally, words of appreciation would not be complete unless they included ones for Don Gingold, a colleague, whose knowledge of publishing proved invaluable in bringing this book to its final stage of publication. To Don, Janet, Lynn, and Jan…thank you!

Two Quotes:

It's almost worth having been in the army for the joy your freedom gives you.

John Dos Passos
American novelist and artist

Above all, Vietnam was a war that asked everything of a few and nothing of most in America.

Myra MacPherson
American author, biographer, and journalist

PREFACE

In 1960, when I first entered college, war was the furthest thing from my mind. John Kennedy had been elected President of the USA and I was focused on simply enjoying college and some day, perhaps, going to Law School. I was thinking about passing the mandatory college Freshman English class at NYU, about majoring in history and economics and taking some political science courses. I was also thinking about life at home, and the long commute from Teaneck New Jersey to my college campus in the Bronx, New York. I was focused on dating, and how lucky I was to be able to afford going to a great private, expensive college.

My parents were middle class and financially struggling and always trying to make ends meet. I had always worked. At 11, I assembled many sections of the New York Times early on Sunday mornings for a pharmacy. At 12, I was stocking shelves at a small, local Grand Union grocery store. This was followed by working in New York City as a stock boy, running errands and mailing parcel post packages containing watches for the Weiler Watch Company. One summer in high school, I took a bus to a nearby town, Ridgefield Park, where I worked as a warehouse worker and union member for a paperboard container manufacturer. I also stocked shelves at Macy's and a coat factory warehouse.

Summer employment was always available although as I grew older, the work became more difficult with back breaking lifting assignments, and continuously changing shift work; no fun and certainly an incentive to do well at school. The pay was good, but not enough to solely pay for NYU. My parents contributed some as did my Aunt Ella and I was awarded a scholarship by my dad's employer. And, still, I needed to get more money. According to my friend, Jim Leopold, this is when I decided to join the Army ROTC program at NYU. Apparently, it paid a stipend reducing tuition.

In 1964, the Communist Vietnamese attacked United States vessels and the President began sending "advisors" to South Vietnam to coach their army on how to stop communism from spreading to that part of the world. The US draft was a way of life and college students wanted to avoid being drafted. My friends all planned to become teachers, or get married and have a child to avoid military service. Receiving a low draft number meant entering the army as a "grunt", rather than being an officer. By being in ROTC, I would serve in the Army as an officer.

I had won a Ford Fellowship to study Political Science in the NYU Washington Square Graduate School so I was thinking seriously of going to Law School. I took the Law Boards to enter Law School. However, Law school was not to be because it was a three year program. The US government agreed to a one year deferment before I was to enter full military service following college graduation. For those too young to know, the war in Vietnam was heating up quickly. The enemy North Vietnamese army, if you could call them an army as they did not fight conventional war, rather a "come and find me" (asymmetrical) tactics, were killing our soldiers in ever larger numbers. The US Congress and the new President were pushing the draft, and inducting men in ever larger numbers.

With the one year deferment, I went to the University of Illinois after learning about their School of Labor and Industrial Relations program. My fraternity brother at NYU had the application and thought the school too far away. I applied and won an assistantship for free tuition, room and board. A year later in an incident described later in this book, I received another half-year deferment to complete a thesis project so I could graduate. That's when I met Janet Drell, the love of my life.

This book begins by describing the first of many unusual occurrences this one taking place between my junior and senior year of college. After taking a bus with other ROTC inductees, my initiation into army life, at Officer Basic Training in Indian Town Gap, Pennsylvania and at Fort Knox Kentucky was rigorous and exhausting Airborne Ranger training. The first of my stories, "The Visit" on a Sunday early in the training cycle sets the stage for a litany of brief stories that relate the strange world surrounding my army life. In total, my stories cover my college experience through the end of my tour of duty. Each story also includes a life lesson drawn from that story's life experience.

The stories are intentionally brief. I hope you find them interesting, easy to read and somewhat thought-provoking. It is only a slice of my life, but I thought worth sharing with kin, friends and others, who would be interested. Enjoy and ponder.

GRIN AND BEAR IT   BY LICHTY

"I know you'll do what's expected of you, Junior! .. Th
Army's a little tougher than we are in that respect!"

THE VISIT

So, it's another dreary day at basic army training camp here near Harrisburg PA. Adding to the dreariness is the pouring rain on this gloomy, cold Sunday. Typical for a Sunday in this summer of 1963, we are all sitting or laying around the barracks with nothing much to do. Thankfully, our drill sergeant is not to be found so some guys are reading in bed in their skivvies while a few others are writing letters to love ones. A couple of guys are spit polishing their shoes. Several fellows are playing cards, (but not for money as none of us really have any money to wager). Water can be heard from hot water showers several future soldiers are taking trying to warm up from the dampness in these barracks.

I am straightening up my footlocker. Suddenly, in bursts the air-borne ranger drill sergeant screaming my name, "STRAUSS, damn it, get into your full uniform and hightail your ass over to the mess hall. Your parents are waiting for you there. You have exactly one and a half hours to get back here". I'm thinking that this is impossible, but an order has been given and I must get myself to the mess hall.

I put on my poncho, head into the driving rain and cross the muddy field to the mess hall. Upon arriving there, to my amazement, there are my parents ready to welcome me with open arms. We embrace and we talk for about 50 minutes. I learn that they took several buses over many hours to get here. I tell them little about my rough life at my basic army training. Suddenly I notice the time, jump up and saying my farewell, instantly leave them for my barracks thinking about what they went through to see me.

Upon returning to my 4th Platoon, I am met by my first sergeant who calls me a "candy ass" for having invited my parents to visit. No sense protesting as he would get the final word anyway. He hands me a toothbrush for my special assignment. As he puts it, "a special privilege like receiving visitors deserves a special assignment"; mine is to clean the toilets for 3 hours on my hands and knees after we "chow down" dinner.

THE LEARNING LESSON: He who receives a wonderful surprise in the military typically pays for it in the end.

SO...WHERE WERE YOU?

It is just past noon on this sunny day. It is November 22nd, 1963. We ROTC cadets are marching around the parade field on our NYU Bronx campus. As usual, I hate it, but better to be in ROTC then take my chances on the draft. With the draft, no one wants to chance going to Vietnam or some other G-d forsaken place as an infantrymen; better to be an officer although statistics say that in combat, officers are usually primary targets of the enemy and die in large numbers.

Suddenly, the commanding officer calls us all to attention and says that we are all dismissed. The reason: The President has been shot and his situation is unknown.

I decide the best place to go is to the newspaper editorial office of *The Heights,* the NYU school newspaper. It will provide the latest AP news releases. Upon getting there, I discover my friend who was the previous year's editor, Dave Merkowitz, and my fraternity brothers from Tau Delta Phi.

We all gather around the AP machine. Together, we decide to remain for the day and publish a special edition of the paper reflecting what is transpiring. We succeed in doing just that, but sadly, we find little comfort in taking it to press. NYU announces school will be cancelled upon notice of President Kennedy's death.

THE LEARNING LESSON: Being busy and staying on top of bad news is no solace for the emotions one feels deep inside; feelings alway percolate to the surface sooner or later. It's only a matter of time.

HOW LUCKY CAN YOU BE?

My days at NYU are rapidly coming to an end and I have taken the Law Boards, but have not applied to any law schools. I have several months to do this as it is still early in my senior year. Still, it is time to make sure that I can get a deferment and go to law school. I communicate with those who make such decisions only to learn that they will NOT grant me that deferment. I ask when it is likely that I will be "called up for duty." I am told it could be up to a year...What to do?

I have a Ford Fellowship and am taking a graduate course at the main downtown NYU campus at Washington Square. The fellowship is in political science which has not been my major. My interest is in Economics and History with a focus on Labor Economics. I had planned to be a Labor Attorney. Now what?

A few days later, I am sitting around the frat house discussing my problem when one of my brothers says that he has considered applying to University of Illinois in Labor-Industrial Relations, but he thinks the school is too far from family, friends and so forth. I ask for his application forms and apply to the school. Several weeks later I learn that I have won a research assistance providing free tuition, room and board. Oh to joy!!! But, one problem...Uncle Sam.

I call and ask for a year's deferment and am told "okay". I am off to a new world of learning, new friends, and new adventures.

THE LEARNING LESSON: Out of apparent uncertainty can come future opportunity and success.

FATE STEPS IN EVEN BIGGER ONCE AGAIN...PART 1

I have been at the University of Illinois for almost a year and have taken all my coursework toward receiving my Masters in Labor-Industrial Relations. It is late August 1965 and I have spent all my time for several summer months slaving over my thesis titled, *Changing Economic and Social Conditions in the Appalachian Region.*

I chose the topic based on the recommendation of my advisor, Professor Gammil in the Economics Department, for whom I had performed many hours of research for my assistantship. He thinks it is a perfect subject because of actions taken by the Kennedy and Johnson Administrations to improve conditions in that impoverished region of the nation, and this is a huge topic of the day.

It is now time to defend the work and present my dissertation by going before the Labor and Industrial Relations School Faculty Board. Upon entering the room and beginning my defense, I am suddenly and most rudely cut off by a faculty member I do not know. It turns out to be Professor Rothstein, who just returned from a sabbatical. He immediately takes the position that the paper is in need of wholesale revision because it fails to emphasize and elaborate how matters are changing in so far as unions are concerned. A major battle ensues between Professor Gammil and Professor Rothstein. Bottom line: The thesis, all 250 plus pages, have to be redone and researched again...no diploma until this is done. Mind you, these are when papers are typed by typewriter and copied in triplicate on onionskin paper.

Now, I need to leave the dorm and relocate someplace. Thank heavens, my grad friends are also relocating to an off-campus apartment. They say I can move in with them temporarily, but one hurtle has yet to be addressed...the Army.

I call and plead my case being given a deferment until early January 1967 to complete my thesis...no later!

THE LEARNING LESSON: Out of controversy can come future happiness.

The Institute of Labor and Industrial Relations at the University of Illinois

Above: Friends in front of grad dorms and (right) house used during grad thesis rewrite.

FATE STEPS IN EVEN BIGGER ONCE AGAIN...PART 2

The fall of 1965 looks to be a really lousy time in my life, one to be filled with doing research and rewriting my thesis.

My colleagues and I are already tired of graduate work having spent the summer attending class, doing research, writing papers, and it is only less than a week into the fall semester. One day, one of them comes up with the idea of calling a friend he had previously dated to see if we could visit her "independent house" to meet the new residents there. After some coaxing, I reluctantly agree to join the fellows heading over there. Lucky for me as this is to be the luckiest day of my life!!!!

Why? Because it is the fateful day I meet my future love and ultimately my future wife, Janet Regina Drell.

At the independent house, Indeco, our eyes meet and we have a wonderful conversation around a coffee table while others talk among themselves. I learn she has transferred in the school's Education Department from the University of Wisconsin. She will be a Junior.

After our first meeting, I ask her out for some ice cream at a Pharmacy that has one of those old-fashioned soda fountain bars. I believe we have another great time, but deep down I wonder if we got serious, what then? I have an Army commitment that I must meet.

In a matter of only 4 months, we get engaged, setting a June date to be married. I must first finish my thesis before getting inducted into the Army. I buy a new Mustang, travel weekly to Campaign-Urbana to see my love or she takes a bus to see me at Fort Benjamin Harrison in Indianapolis. My life has made a HUGE TRANSITION.

THE LEARNING LESSON: Life changes quickly and one can never anticipate what life has in store for us.

FORT BEN HARRISON, ADJUDANT GENERAL SCHOOL

Nothing like receiving orders to relocate when you have no control over where your future assignment location will be. Fortunately, for me, my orders are for me to go to Fort Benjamin Harrison, Indiana, a relatively small post in the Indianapolis area. I am part of a contingent of new officers there to be schooled over a few months in the ways of the army.

We suffer through Army classes, gas mask training by heading through gas filled rooms while wearing a gas mask with lots of coughing and choking after or head to Fort Knox, not to look at the gold stored there, but through a "field of fire" exercise called "The Field Infiltration Course". This entails wearing army fatigues, no other outer clothing, (with the temps at about 30 degrees) and going down on my belly with rifle in hand, crawling a hundred yards through a water soaked muddy field with barbed wire strung 6 inches overhead while live bullets streak across the field some 8-12 inches above my head. What fun!

What makes all this tolerable is the opportunity to see my sweetheart, Jan, soon to be fiancee. She is in Champaign/Urbana Illinois some 120 miles away. With my first paycheck in hand, a classmate and I negotiate the purchase of 2 identical 19641/2 Ford Mustangs. On the following weekend, it is time to go to Illinois. It proves to be a wonderful trip, one that would be repeated every other weekend while at Fort Harrison.

On the following Monday morning, upon returning to class, I ask my fellow student how his new Mustang was driving (as we were told to hold the speed under 40 MPH for the first 100 miles). He replies, "I was never able to find out." I said, "What do you mean"? His reply, "I never got a mile off post before being hit broadside at the first inter-section off post. My car was totaled, but I came away with only bruises. I am totally covered by my insurance, and have put in an order for an identical replacement Mustang. 3 identical Mustangs sold to us…that's what I call a very lucky car dealer!"

THE LEARNING LESSON: Fate plays a big role in our lives. You can plan short and long term, but always have a PLAN B in mind.

Picture: Fort Benjamin Harrison's main building.

THIS BACHELOR'S NEW LIFE

I am assigned to Fort Bliss, Texas. I am a Lieutenant in charge of a large portion of an Army Reception Station, not a local recruiting station at a mall where a small staff tries to convince perspective high school kids to join the military. No... this place is enormous. It consists of huge armory-like building where hundreds of new recruits take various tests ranging from IQ to manual dexterity tests. 48,000 men per month take these tests.

From three days of testing, each new soldier is given a Military Occupational Specialty (MOS) and their future assignments post-basic training. I am in charge of the Testing and Evaluation section that gives the tests, scores them, then sends the information to the Pentagon for determination of each MOS. Dozens of men serve as my staff.

Living in my own barracks room, I am befriended by a Captain (Ron Vincent). Jan and I are engaged to marry in June and it is now springtime in desert country. Ron is a rather heavy-set fellow, very gregarious and fun loving. I am busy with my duties, writing and calling Jan, watching TV in a shared congregational-type relaxation room, and occasionally going to the movies nearby. In other words, I am biding time until Jan joins me.

This Captain is always after me to join him on one of his Sunday adventures traveling into the desert. He typically travels down well-paved roads and then off-roads onto dirt roads to see where they will lead. The unusual thing about this is that his car is a very small MG roadster. The first time I go with him, we follow a mountain pass. We then hike about a mile and discover a very old Indian structure (my guess, several hundred years old). We discover remains of an old fire-pit and remnants of corn. We leave everything behind as we found them. Apparently, no one has discovered these for decades and I doubt we also could find them again.

THE LEARNING LESSON: Army life, absolutely, moves a person down paths of discovery never anticipated. This will prove true time and again!

A TRULY STRANGE ADVENTURE AWAITS: PART 1

On a gloriously beautiful Sunday, Ron convinces me to again join him for an new adventure. Ron says we should be back well before dinner. With nothing much better to do, I accept.

We leave the post about 8 a.m. and travel for about two hours. Ron suddenly pulls off the highway and takes out his map. He says that he strongly believes that he can find this old ghost town about 3-4 mile off the roadway. It is getting hot, but not to worry, we have plenty of water and some sandwiches.

Ron turns the car onto this gravel road and we proceed along this dry riverbed. The road rapidly decays into dirt, sand, and larger rocks. Mind you, we are in a small MG roadster with the top down. The ride is getting bumpier with each 1/4 mile traveled.

I question the sanity of this venture and state that we probably should turn around. It is now about high noon, but Ron argues it is only a short distance further. We stop, eat in the shade of the car, and then proceed. By 1 p.m., it is obvious that Ron is wrong. Hesitantly, he turns the car around. I feel fried.

As we travel the road bed, we both see it...a 6-7 foot rattle snake sunny himself 25-30 feet across our path. There are boulders around, but I can picture a way around the snake and say as much. Ron will have none of it and guns the engine driving straight for the snake. The snake is run over, and I can see in the rear mirror that he has coiled as if to strike. I think farewell, but NO...Ron has other ideas. He spins the car around and guns for the snake. The snake strikes at the car and is thrown OVER US onto the back trunk of the car. He slides off. Ron spins the car around again to strike at the snake. The snake gives up and moves quickly under a boulder. What insanity!

THE LEARNING LESSON: Some folks love extreme adventuring. Not me.

A Bachelor's life: Traveling around Texas in an MG Roadster

THE STRANGE ADVENTURE CONTINUES: PART 2

Not more than a half hour after the snake encounter, while proceeding down the riverbed, Ron's MG roadster hits a big rock and bang, his pedal control is shot. The car continues to proceed forward at about 5 miles per hour on its own without anyone stepping on the floor pedal. To stop the car, Ron has to pull the emergency brake. Upon releasing it, the car immediately moves forward again on its own at 5 miles per hour.

Again, the car brake is applied and Ron scoots under the car to see if he can fix the problem...no dice. No choice; hop in the car and SLOWLY limp back to Fort Bliss, some 40-45 miles away.

At 10:15 p.m., without dinner, exhausted or spent and burnt out, we arrive back at base.

THE LEARNING LESSON: DO NOT join crazy guys off-roading in cars with low chaises!

P.S. This lesson was reinforced and learned again many years later when with friends, we stop at a scenic overlook near Jackson Hole, WY; I learn if there is a rock strewn about, a car with a low chassis (like mine) will be driven over it and the rock will be sure to puncture the oil pan.

Jan and Don get Married!!!!

NEWLYWEDS DISCOVER ARMY LIFE

Following a long, arduous trip from Rockford, Illinois, we arrive in our new hometown, El Paso, Texas. We stay at a lovely little hotel and awaken to the sounds of birds chirping. Upon going outside, we see our first hummingbirds. What a great omen for the future.

At Fort Bliss, we are surprised to learn that we will be given a two bedroom house to be furnished by Uncle Sam. We are given keys to the house and then toured through a warehouse where furniture is stacked high. We are told to identify any furniture that we would like. It will be delivered to our house. Wow...that was easy. We also go out to a wholesale-type store near the Mexico border and purchase our king bed, a blue couch, and two matching barrel chairs for immediate delivery to our new house.

We go to the PX, and marvel at the price of food, a fraction of what we expected to pay. Milk, bread, staples cost mere pennies.

Jan learns to drive the stick shift on our Mustang as she has to drive up a huge mountain to get to campus after enrolling at Texas Western College (who take the national Basketball championship that year). The school has a beautiful campus and she quickly learns to navigate her way there.

Over a year's time, straight sunny days, typical for El Paso and more to come. Every day brings another fun morning with Jan, as well as lovely evenings, cheap movies, and salutes to Jan and me whenever we enter the army post and also around town because a sticker identifies the car as belonging to an officer. There are weekend trips to the mountains in Las Cruces, NM and to Carlsbad NM to see the bats and caves, as well as out to Tombstone, Arizona and Santa Fe and Albuquerque, N.M.

Jan's folks come to pay us a short visit. We meet the Jewish community who live on top of the mountain. They welcome us, even going so far as to offer me a job in real estate when I get out of the Army.

THE LEARNING LESSON: Whoever says that Army life as an officer stateside is bad, is nuts; it can be terrific.

NOT YOUR TYPICAL "DUTY OFFICER" DAILY ROSTER

It is my turn to be "Officer of the Day", a role assigned to every officer on a rotating basis. It is a Sunday evening, I bid farewell to Jan until the next morning as this duty will take me through the night until the following day's roster ("Morning/Daily Report") is submitted which in this case is on Monday morning.

This is typically pretty much a ho-hum responsibility, watching TV with a private and a sergeant, drinking coffee, and trying to keep one of us awake until the following morning when I am expected to turn in the "Daily Report" which profiles anything that happens during the night.

At 6:53 p.m., two soldiers knock on the recreation room screen door. One is throwing up outside and the other also claims to be ill. I tell my private to take the jeep and drive these soldiers to the infirmary by the hospital.

At 7:05 p.m., two new soldiers appear. One is doubled over in pain and the other claims to have severe stomach cramps. As my sergeant and I are discussing his going over to fetch another jeep, 3 other sick soldiers appear I tell the sergeant to get our panel truck and take them all to the infirmary.

As soon as he departs and the private returns, 4 more soldiers claim similar symptoms. I tell him to get a "deuce and a half" vehicle which can carry over 20 men. By the time he returns, 6 other soldiers appear from the barracks. All are sick, a few doubled over in pain. I tell the private to take everyone to the hospital emergency room so the hospital staff can better assess the situation and determine the cause of this outbreak.

My sergeant is back at 8:30 p.m. and secures another large vehicle. We shove new arrivals onto that vehicle…and so it goes over and over again for another eight hours. I write the name and symptoms of every soldier on the "Morning/Daily Report" before sending them to the hospital.

THE LEARNING LESSON: Following written protocol and using common sense usually shields a person from being accused of stupidity.

POSTSCRIPT: SO WHAT HAPPENED WITH MY UNTYPICAL "DUTY OFFICER" DAILY ROSTER

At 7 a.m. sharp, I knock on the Major's door, enter, salute, and state that I am submitting the Morning Report. He takes my 20 page report (typically one page) filled with hundreds of names. He screams out about 10 choice curse words. He asks me why I hadn't called him during the night and I truthfully tell him that we handled the emergency cases as they arose, no reason to bother him on a lovely Sunday evening. All in a day's work!

Next, the Inspector General is called in to do a full investigation of what prompted the incident. Mind you, our Army Reception Station feeds about 4000 men at every meal, which includes recent inductees going through basic army training, plus German soldiers assigned to neighboring White Sands Missile Testing Range for missile training.

Sunday night is "cold cuts and salads" night to relieve the kitchen staff from preparing hot meals like those provided the remaining six nights of the week. On this particular weekend, someone really screwed up. They failed to refrigerate the potato salad that was made and cooled in large 10 gallon pots to a required cold temperature. Because of this, harmful bacteria grew in the food causing over 400 soldiers to become sick with Ptomaine Poisoning. Some soldiers were so sick, it took days before they could be released from the hospital.

THE LEARNING LESSON: Salmonella and E. Coli infections are brutal and can run havoc to us humans. Food spoilage is always possible, yet it is preventable. Accidents happen so "an ounce of prevention is worth a thousand cures".

Below: I swear in new recruits.

OF ABRAHAM LINCOLN AND THE OAK LEAF CLUSTER

Under my command over some 8 months, my team has processed about 32,000 men into the army through the Fort Bliss Army Reception Station. We had administered inoculations, given uniforms and footlockers, housed and feed them and tested all these individuals, assigning each soldier a Military Occupational Specialty, i.e. better known as an MOS. For those individuals scoring well on tests, we discussed their eligibility for Officer's Candidate School. Some decided to pursue this option, others said "No".

Sometime in January 1967, the Army Reception Station's ranking officer, one Abraham Lincoln, calls me and another Lieutenant into his office. After saluting and going through the preliminary welcoming, Colonel Lincoln comes to the point saying, "Lieutenants. I called you in here to congratulate you both on the operations of the Reception Station. You have done a superlative job leading your organizations. We set records for outstanding performance by all measures. I am rewarding each of you with the honor of the Army Commendation Metal". The medal is awarded to American military personnel who perform noteworthy service in their capacity to the United States Army. Qualifying service for the award of the medal is for "distinctive meritorious achievement and performance of duty".

Lieutenant Tindle and I thank the Colonel for the honor. Then the Colonel says, "I am sending a message to the Pentagon informing them of this stellar service". Upon hearing this, the other Lieutenant and I both speak up and recommend that this not be done fearing that notifying the Pentagon will raise our profile which, in turn, could result in who knows what. "Nonsense", said the Colonel, "You both are being too reserved". The Colonel will not be dissuaded from his plan.

Sure enough, not even four days later, the Colonel calls us in to apologize, telling us we have new orders and are to report to Fort Riley Kansas for new assignments.

THE LEARNING LESSON: No good deed goes unanswered in one way or another in the US Army.

CITATION

THE ARMY COMMENDATION MEDAL

is awarded to

First Lieutenant DONALD C. STRAUSS, 05019200, Adjutant General's Corps, United States Army, for meritorious service in consecutive assignments as Chief of the Officer Candidate School Enlistment Section and the Classification and Testing Branch, United States Army Reception Station, United States Army Training Center (Air Defense), United States Army Air Defense Center, Fort Bliss, Texas, for the period 1 April 1966 to 16 January 1967. Although impeded by a constant shortage of experienced personnel and non-availability of directives and precedence, he invariably insured attainment of the objectives of the sections under his supervision. Through zealous initiative and diligence he organized and established proficient operations and capably implemented the officer candidate school program. He assisted immeasurably in the development of an effective classification and assignment system which enabled the United States Army Reception Station to accomplish its mission in a highly commendable manner. He capably developed and instituted methods to provide continuity of operations and effect high standards of performance. His professional competence, mature judgment and perseverance are in keeping with the highest traditions of the United States Army and reflect great credit upon First Lieutenant Strauss and the military service.

All our possessions head off to Kansas in our 1964 1/2 Mustang; no moving truck or trailer:

KANSAS...DARK AND COLD

Hard to imagine, but true...a couple can pack all their possessions of about six months of marriage into a small 19641/2 Ford Mustang. We drive 822 miles to our destination, with house plants and an ironing board strapped to the vehicle's roof. What a picture!

It only takes two days of driving, to reach our new assigned local; however, it is like going from paradise to hell. Jan and I leave the beautiful desert and relative warm climate of 60+ temperature days of sun in January (El Paso had over 3 years of consecutive sunny days) for bone chilling cold, snowy Junction City Kansas, the location of Fort Riley.

We leave behind beautiful memories of days visiting fun and lovely sites such as Las Cruces, New Mexico; Albuquerque, New Mexico, Tombstone, Arizona; Carlsbad Caverns, Texas, among other locations.

It isn't long as we drive through the Texas panhandle before we encounter blowing snow which fortunately, doesn't accumulate to much. We drove on and two evenings later, we enter Fort Riley. We ask the whereabouts of the officer's club/barracks. Upon arriving, we enter a night duty officer's lounge and see everyone gathered around the television. What we see and hear on the TV is news of three Apollo Astronauts dying in a launching pad flash fire. They are Virgil I. Grissom, 40 years old, Air Force Lieutenant Colonel, one of the seven original Mercury astronauts, Edward H. White II, 36, a Lieutenant Colonel in the Air Force, the first American to "walk" in space, and Roger P. Chaffee, 31, a Navy Lieutenant Commander, who has been awaiting his first space flight.

We are given keys, and told where to sleep. Sadly, we then again unload our possessions from the Mustang and turn in for the night, not knowing what will await us over the days to come.

THE LEARNING LESSON: Enjoy life one day at a time as part of life's adventure; no telling what awaits us.

AN UNUSUAL MIXTURE: OF BUFFALOS, CARVEL, ENCYCLOPEDIAS, AND THE TOPEKA TORNADO

On our first day in Junction City Kansas and Fort Riley, we learned that it had been the home of the "Big Red 1", the 1st Infantry Division of the US Army. This translated into thousands of fighting men and women and their families who had lived on the post and surrounding area. In the summer of 1966, the Big Red 1 became the first division-sized organization deployed to fight in Vietnam.

And there we are, the new arrivals, here to train and eventually deploy somewhere overseas. My unit is to be called the 38th BPO (Base Postal Organization), whatever that is supposed to mean. Before reporting to the unit, Jan and I are given a few days to find housing and unpack. We soon learn this means that we are to use this enormous key ring with hundreds of keys, choose whatever garden apartment we want after journeying through abandoned apartments. We can also choose whatever abandoned furniture we can move into our new apartment. What a joke!

So starts our new lifestyle…weird and seriously depressing. No friends… only a TV for entertainment, and other than driving to see buffalos grazing on the Fort's campgrounds, our entertainment consists of walking a few blocks nightly to a Carvel stand for ice cream (despite it being the cold middle of winter). And oh yes, Jan's purchase of a set of encyclopedias that she thinks we should have to learn more about the world.

What of weekends? There aren't any free days other than one weekend where we travel to Topeka Kansas to see the devastation wrought upon the city the previous summer by the first tornado in U.S. history to exceed $100 million in damage, with a Fujita Scale rating of F5. It had a ground path of 22 miles through the city, killing 16 people, injuring over 500, destroying 820 homes and damaging 3000. We observe how it had traveled straight through the City Municipal Building. We take a picture or two, one of a bus that had been upended to stand on its front bumpers. No joy in Kansas!

THE LEARNING LESSON: Tough times can bring newlyweds together with small pleasures (as it does in our case).

The non-fun times at Fort Riley, Kansas…January-March 1967

PREPARING FOR DEPLOYMENT THE ARMY WAY

The telephone rings and it is 3:30 a.m., waking us up. It is pitch dark and the temperature outside is about zero. The call is to get my canteen, rifle, backpack with rations and miscellaneous supplies and hightail it to a staging area for war games in the great outdoors. Yippee! I turn to Jan after getting into my fatigues and jacket and say "I should be back by late breakfast. No one is crazy enough to stay out in this cold". Since we are training for overseas deployment under these conditions, I think we will be going to Korea, not Vietnam, after our organization proves itself ready for deployment.

An hour later, I am lying in a field at the base of a small 3-4 foot knoll. I try desperately to dig a small foxhole or trench, but the ground is rock solid because it is totally frozen. Over the knoll some 75 yards away is a thicket or stand of trees. Beyond that, I can see a few "enemy helicopters" touching down and taking off. My team is embedded some 20 yards on each side of me, but we honestly don't have much cover. In the distance within these "war games", I can hear ongoing battles and machine gun fire. It's is about as close to real war as I want to get.

I wait and try to get some shut eye, but it is freezing with a nasty wind and the hard ground that gives no relief. It is well over an hour until dawn. Another hour passes and my hands feel a bit numb in my gloves. I worry that some of my troops will suffer frost bite if we remain outdoors much longer. The sky brightens, but dawn remains almost a half hour away. I hear louder noises in the distance beyond the tree line. For certain, they are getting louder; still I see nothing out there. The water has frozen solid in my canteen. When will they call an end to all this?

All of a sudden, dozens of enemy soldiers come out of tree line. Machine gun fire is also coming forth and tanks are coming at us at full throttle. Holy cow...one is coming straight at me. I roll and roll sideways and see the tank tracks pass within yards of me. I get to my feet and scramble to get the hell out of there while yelling for us to take a retrograde maneuver.

THE LEARNING LESSON: You cannot imagine the fear when in battle.

ONE OF MY LUCKIEST OF DAYS

With training coming to end and the unit in it's final days of packing and preparing for deployment, I am physiologically ready to leave with my unit. But then comes the big surprise!

While talking to a few other officers, Major Stinger drops in and interrupts, saying, "Lieutenant, I have nominated you for Jungle School. You should be receiving orders to depart for Panama in a few days".

Jungle School is in Panama, Central America. It is the training school that teaches how to fight hand-to-hand in gorilla-style warfare. Yikes, I am thinking…not a place that I want to go to.

I am told, after some level of training, an individual is dropped off alone on a Panama Caribbean beach by oneself armed only with a knife and a compass. Only the jungle lies ahead and exists all the way to the Pacific Ocean where you are expected to arrive in a certain number of days. You are given no food or shelter. It's up to you to forage for days through the undergrowth and find your way to the destination where you will be picked up by an awaiting submarine. What fun!!!

My head is spinning; this can't be happening to me.

To my amazement, a fellow Lieutenant says, "Shit, I wish I could go; it's a school I always wanted to attend". Major Stinger is as much in disbelief as I am, but quickly regains his natural scowl and says, "If that's what you want, than that's what you will get. I'll alert the Pentagon to this new discussion. Strauss, expect a change to your orders; no Jungle School for you".

THE LESSON LEARNED: The "fickle finger of fate" has interceded on my behalf. Life is filled with many bad and good moments, but rarely do they occur so quickly together as in my case. When good moments follow bad ones, it feels doubly great!

THE GREAT JOURNEY: PART 1. FLYING TO THE MYSTERY CRUISE

Hard to believe, but in only some 8 weeks, under Major Stinger (who I despise), my organization of some 130 strangers has been shaped into a hard core, efficient team or organization that can get things done. We are told that we will deploy for overseas in a matter of days. I am told that I will be in charge with two long-experienced sergeants in getting the entire outfit to our mystery destination. Our Major and a Lieutenant Scully will fly in advance with a few soldiers to ensure facilities are prepared for our arrival.

On the last day before our departure, Major Stinger calls for a formation and announces that two of our men have written to their Senators or Congressmen complaining about the unreasonable treatment they have endured. The Major indicates that the two men will not be joining the unit for deployment, but will be reassigned to another unit on post that also will be departing for parts unknown (more on these soldiers later in this book).

On the final night before we all leave Fort Riley, the Major invites us officers and wives to the Officer's Club for cocktails and dinner. It turns out to be one round after another of drinking Singapore Slings. By the time we all leave the club, we are all totally soused.

The next day, Jan and I say our goodbyes, never to know if or when we will be together again.   She leaves for Illinois and I go off to a local airfield to take an army air transport via Denver to San Francisco with a hundred plus of my kindred soldiers.

Upon arrival in San Francisco, we are all whisked off to the seaport where we are transferred onto an enormous transport ship. I learn the ship was used to transport men from Europe after World War II, to and from Korea, and now again to who knows where…our secret destination. The next day, I am slipping and sliding through vomit as thousands of men are sick have seasickness after floating under the Golden Gate Bridge. That night, my new bunkmate, above me, pukes down into a pan inches from my head.

THE LEARNING LESSON: Military life is no picnic & provides no choices.

Leaving San Francisco
and home at sea.

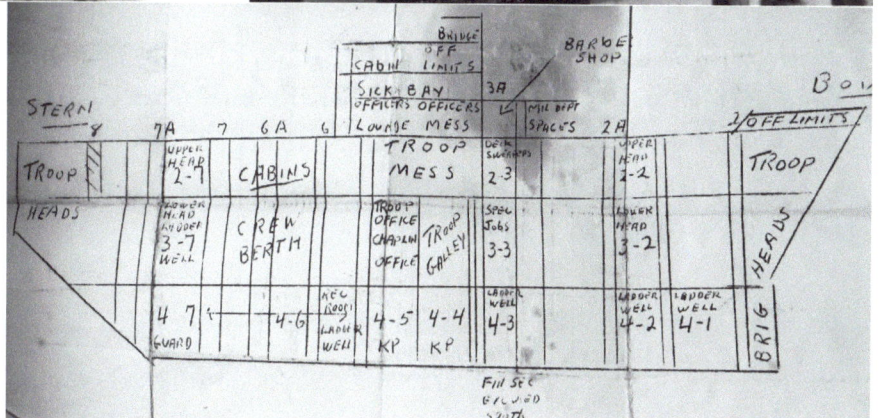

25

THE GREAT JOURNEY: PART 2. THE PHILIPPINES AND SUBIC BAY

After twenty eight days upon the sea, I observe the ship slowly floating amongst the most beautiful islands that a person can imagine. True rain forests extend to the water's edge. On occasion, I see a house or two on stilts and a child or two waving in the distance, in addition to small boats pulled up on tiny beaches. Imagine, the excitement of all on board seeing this revelation. We are moving amongst various, small Philippine Islands.

Several hours later, we dock at Subic Bay, the Philippines. We await orders, but none initially are forthcoming. I grab my camera and wait on the deck. Lo and behold, to my chagrin and amazement enters Major Stinger, my nemesis. I am thinking, what is he doing and how did he get here? Shortly, thereafter, I learn that he has flown in from Vietnam, our destination, and he is here to lead us the rest of the way, through part of a day in Subic Harbor and then into Vietnam. Shit!

We are given shore leave for several hours. I plan to take a few pictures and buy a few things. I am told by Major Stinger to be at the Officer's Club in an hour. I take a few photos and have a colleague take a few of me. I purchase a few Philippine artists' paintings to be sent to Jan, and find that is all the time I have to pursue my interests. Off to the Officers' Club I go.

Upon entering the club, I am called over to a table where my two unit sergeants are sitting with Major Stinger. He is embroiled in an argument with the club's management over the presence of the sergeants in the club. The management says the sergeants have a club of their own to go to. The Major, who in Korea was a sergeant promoted in the field to officer rank, says these sergeants are heading to Vietnam, and if the management wants a fight, he and his men, including me, will smash their faces in. It is obvious the Major has already had his fill of liquor. The club authorities back off and in celebration, the Major calls for many shots of beer and whiskey, and then commands us all to drink one round after another. So, ends my opportunity to go sightseeing. The sergeants have to carry the Major back to the ship and he is restricted to his bay for several days.

THE LEARNING LESSON: Military life, as all of life, continually provides us with good and bad surprises.

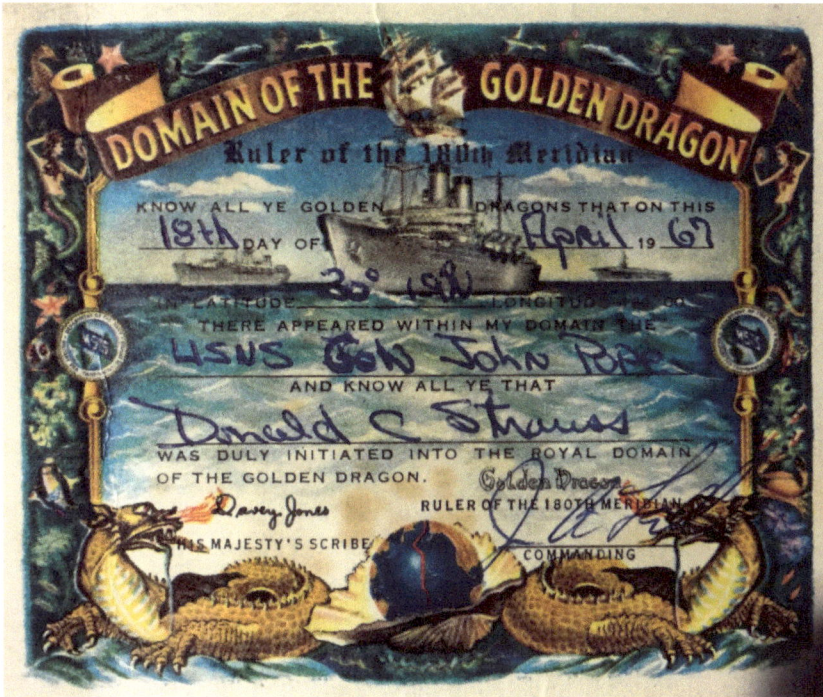

28 days at sea, crossing the International date line and a few short hours in Subic Bay, the Philippines.

THE GREAT JOURNEY: PART 3. GOTTLIEB & THE ROASTED EGGS

Day after day we travel across the Pacific Ocean. We sit on the deck and talk and stare out at the sea. We decide that we are destined to go either to Vietnam or Korea, one destination could be okay, the other not so. The men below are rarely given the opportunity to be on deck. They get into arguments, fights and bets playing card games amongst themselves. Bottom line: it's no fun, but it could be worse. Boredom beats war.

We pass through days of glorious sunshine, days of gray ominous clouds, and on one occasion, a storm that requires everything be held down as dinner plates get tossed around while passing through rough seas. And then, there are the occasional porpoises that follow the ship as we gently move onward at our speed of about 14 knots per hour.

About several weeks at sea, I am asked if I am Jewish. I answer in the affirmative and am asked if I and any other Jewish soldiers in my unit would care to join the Captain's second in command, a fellow named Gottlieb, for a Passover Seder. It seems completely crazy that here I am in the middle of the Pacific Ocean heading for who knows where and I am attending a Seder. But, the truth be told, this is to take place.

We are a group of about 15 taking turns reading from a Haggadah. Just before we stop to eat dinner, in walks a steward with a large platter filled with a foot high pile of roasted (not boiled) inedible eggs. Gottlieb asks the steward, "What's the meaning of this?" and the steward replies, "You asked for a roasted egg and so here they are". To which Gottlieb replies, "I asked for A roasted egg, not dozens of eggs. Whatever made you think I needed all these eggs which in fact, are inedible?" Replies the steward, "It's not my holiday so I don't know why you need such an egg. I thought perhaps each person should have his own egg…if nothing else, they could be a memento of the occasion". And with that, we all begin to chuckle, which under the circumstances leads to large belly laughs as we all think about the ridiculousness of the situation.

THE LEARNING LESSON: When bored, yet, stressed to the max (not knowing one's future), it doesn't take much to see how absurd certain occurrences can be.

THE GREAT JOURNEY: PART 4: VIETNAM. A BIZARRE BEGINNING

I thought I had seen a lot in my young lifetime, but life is to prove even more surprising. Docking our ship in Soc Trang, Vietnam was another eye opening experience. I can see that we are at the base of a river that snakes inland and there is a small city beyond the harbor.

No sooner than we are docked that I observe from the deck, many feet down at the water line. All manner of cargo is being taken off the ship, yet no men are being off-loaded. Additionally, I observe frogmen diving off the PT boats into the water and setting off depth charges that reverberate throughout the hull of the ship. What in the world are they doing?

The answer to the question is: Security and Prevention. The frogman are dropping depth charges to prevent Viet Cong coming up alongside or submerging under our ship and placing explosive mines on it. Hard to believe our ship is vulnerable to being sunk here until it leaves port. Not surprising…I now know for sure that I have entered a dangerous place, i.e. a war zone.

THE LEARNING LESSON: A lesson for life…One need not seek out danger as it is almost always present, although not always obvious. Unlike life in Soc Trang, danger often appears suddenly in most surprising ways.

THE GREAT JOURNEY: PART 5: STORM THE BEACHES

Our huge troop ship now drops anchor approximately 200 yards from the coastline and gently floats above the 3-4 foot, small swells that lap its bulk. Rope ladders are tossed over the sides and we are told to get our weapon and gear and get ready for an amphibious landing onto the beaches of Vietnam. I think, you must be kidding, but no, this is what is to happen!

After 28 days on the Pacific Ocean and it comes down to going over the side with my backpack and weapon, descending down an 80+ foot rope ladder, hand-over-hand. I am helped onto a landing craft and soon, when filled with men, the engines come alive and we are transported toward the beach. At about 150 feet out, we are told to get out and attack the beach a la the Omaha Beach landing, even though it took place some 23 years earlier. I am up to by shoulders in warm water with my M-16 held high over my head as I slog through the water to the shoreline.

Some 8-10 minutes later, I drop onto the beach with others on both sides of me. The beach is about 75 feet wide and in the distance beyond that, I see men waving to us to get up and walk to them…no shots fired, just soldiers standing by deuce-and-a-half trucks awaiting our arrival. We are told to climb onto the trucks to be taken to our destination in Vietnam. So, we pack onto the truck and are driven for what seems like a few hours through the countryside inside a very hot vehicle covered with its canvas tarps in virtual darkness.

I surmise that I can look forward to a number of weird and difficult coming months in a place far from home. Welcome to Vietnam!

THE LEARNING LESSON: By any definition, life can be difficult, but there are folks who want to make it more so for the unsuspecting. Is it to get their "jollies", to somehow get even for a past wrong, to teach a cynical lesson, or is it their "human nature" that brings out the "dark side"?

LSTs to get us to land on the beaches of Vung Tau.

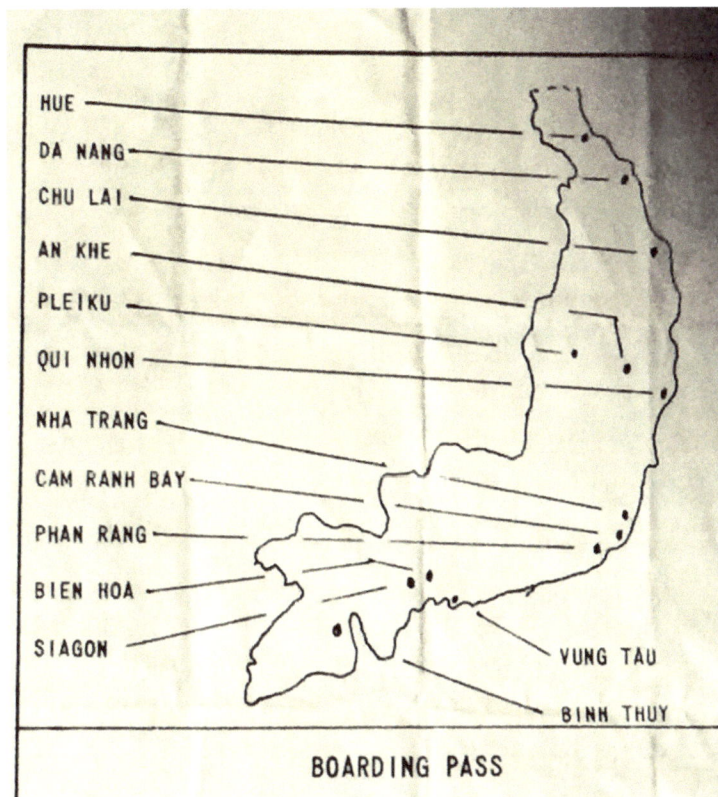

HUE
DA NANG
CHU LAI
AN KHE
PLEIKU
QUI NHON
NHA TRANG
CAM RANH BAY
PHAN RANG
BIEN HOA
SIAGON
VUNG TAU
BINH THUY

BOARDING PASS

WELCOME TO YOUR NEW HOME

They say, "Home is where the heart is", but truthfully, I am not going to describe my new residence in that way. The name of the place is called "Camp Red Ball", and quite an interesting place it is. It can best be described as a compound surrounded by 10 foot fencing topped off with razor wire. There is an iron gate that can be opened to accommodate large vehicles at the entrance. Next to the gate is a 25 foot high guard tower.

Imagine a perimeter around a prison and then picture a compound that is about a football field in circumference. Looking into the compound from the front gate to my left are three very large two story wooden barracks. Besides these barracks, but against a back fence are some one story cement barracks (sleeping quarters for officers). To my right, on the other side of the compound are four wooden structures along the fence line. The one closest to the gate is a roofed drinking bar, which has an open side facing toward the barracks. Next to it, is a long enclosed building which again has large door openings that face the barracks across the large open field. it will be our Base Post Office. The third building toward the back of the fence is a fully enclosed smaller structure that will be described later as the "Personal Effects Depot". The fourth building is our cafeteria/mess hall.

Camp Red Ball is about 10 kilometers outside Tan Son Nhat Airport which sits at the northern end of Saigon, Vietnam. Our camp sits next to a small housing area and is joined to the airport via a long, dirt road. Just outside the bar area on the other side of the fence sits dilapidated wooden buildings which serve as brothels. At the back of the compound sit open rice paddies with three foot sandbag walls at the base of the fence line.

My room consists of a twin bed with 5 foot high wooden posts that are there to hold mosquito netting so I am not bitten to death during the night. There are also a few foot lockers and a rack to hold one's clothing and personal belongings. It is a 10 by perhaps 10 foot room with another doorway at the rear that holds a private poured cement cold water shower and sink basin, both growing a turf of green algae. So this is my new home!

THE LEARNING LESSON: Be happy with your lot in life; mosquitos, green algae, barbed wire…it could be worse in the infantry or artillery.

Camp Red Ball: The building with my room, my bed, and the compound's open field.

Neighboring kids just outside our compound's barbed wire fence.

OF STEVEDORES AND THE "PARIS OF THE EAST".

Forget western-like cities. Instead, picture a third world city, much like one would see anywhere outside the USA; shops with gates to protect against thievery at night. There are pretty two story private homes behind walls, bridges over rivers and canals filled with river craft, generally floating 8-10 foot dingy-like vessels. There also are alleys, parks, and interesting sidewalk peddlers. The streets are filled with thousands of motor bikes. About half convey two people; often a women sitting sidesaddle holding on while carrying groceries, plants, and so forth. You will also see street merchants everywhere peddling their wares, often food in two big pots joined by a pole that a person would carry across their shoulder.

Well, that's Saigon, the "Paris of the East", a city where I now find myself on a daily basis. Not that I am a stranger to big cities having grown up near New York. As in all cities, you have to know where safe and unsafe places are and you need to make sure that you are in the right places. Why, "Paris of the East"? Because of the French influence on architecture, (shops with awnings), as well as many "French" restaurants.

Forget my education in Human Resource Management. Instead, picture me managing stevedores unloading conex containers (those large boxes that can sit on trailers or lifted onto trains or stacked high on ships). Indeed, that's the reason for my daily trips to the huge docks of Saigon. There I yell orders for the offloading of these containers by cranes from very large Sea-land Container Ships from the USA. I learn how to climb all over ships from many stories down deep in their hulls to hundreds of feet up on top of stacks of these containers. Life is one of finding containers by the number stenciled on them, often like finding "a needle in a haystack". Then I have it plucked and deposited on truck frames for transit to our postal depot at Camp Red Ball.

THE LEARNING LESSON: It's like learning how to swim by being tossed into deep water for the first time…fear quickly evaporates when having to survive, as in my case, in new and strange places.

Top left: Saigon Harbor
Top right: New military harbor.
Below left: schematic of ship to be unloaded. Other photos: into the bowels of the ship to lift conexs full of mail off the ship.

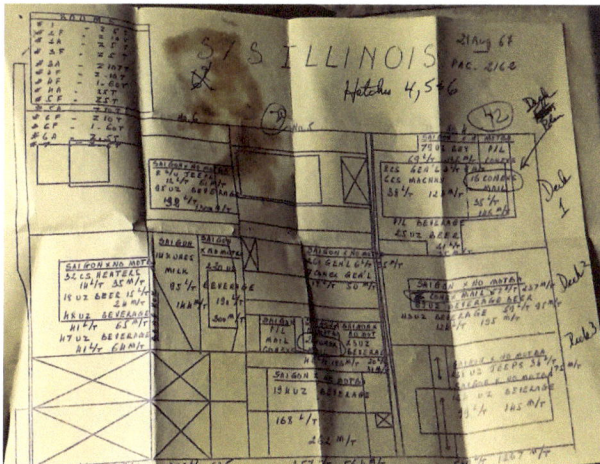

LIFE IN THE 38TH BASE POSTAL ORGANIZATION (BPO)

So what does the 38th BPO do and why is it situated at Camp Red Ball?

The 38th BPO is the name given to the unit of men that I took by plane and ship to Vietnam. It is comprised of about 130 men whose responsibility is to get all parcel post mail; boxes filled with sox, salamis, Jello Shake-up puddings, candy, all manner of clothing and non-perishable food, to our soldiers in the territory where they reside, i.e. the lower half of southern Vietnam. My role is to get the cargo containers with these parcels off the ships after they crossed the Pacific Ocean.

Containers are sent to our outpost, Camp Red Ball, on the outskirts of Saigon, about 10 kilometers outside the city proper. There we break open the seal to the container, remove the contents, move them into our warehouse where the packages are sorted into mailbags, and removed back onto deuce-and-a-half vehicles. From there, our drivers transport the packages to their destinations throughout the country.

Shifts typically are 8-10 hours and most men spend their evenings drinking themselves silly. Curfew is at 11 p.m. and if a soldier can manage transportation, they can leave for distances unknown, but that is seldom done. More typically, some soldiers find their way to the neighboring brothels. Guess who has to go get them when they fail to show during bed check? You guessed it…me and another officer; accompanied by one of my sergeants and sometimes, one or two others. Often, it is difficult convincing them to return; and more difficult having to carry their drunken bodies back to the base camp.

We wondered, "Where is the enemy"? It seems like the Viet Cong like to play games with us. For example, they boobytrapped one of our latrines. The trip-wire was set off accidentally by a native women's mop when she went to use it. Fortunately, she was unhurt.

THE LEARNING LESSON: You do the unusual jobs asked of you because you know there are months of living that crazy life ahead of you; anticipating getting out of a war zone would drive you insane. Take life one day at a time,

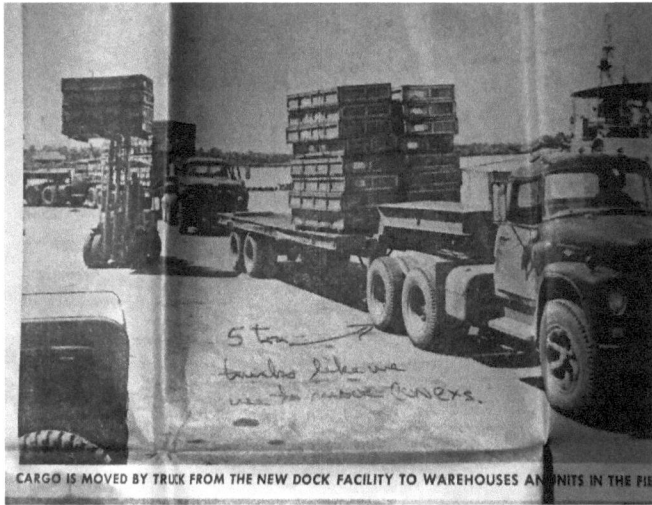

CARGO IS MOVED BY TRUCK FROM THE NEW DOCK FACILITY TO WAREHOUSES AND UNITS IN THE PIER

Mail travels in conexs from ships to Camp Red Ball where they are stacked, then unloaded and re-sorted. Next, mail is put on our trucks for transport to various destinations throughout the southern part of Vietnam.

OF METAL BOXES, AND PERSONAL EFFECTS

As described earlier, Camp Red Ball has a large open gravel field in the middle of this property. Initially, that space is vacant, but not for long. It is only a matter of days following my trips to the harbor before our cargo containers start to occupy the space. These boxes are removed and transported back to the harbor by my men as fast as possible, but there are always about a dozen boxes waiting to be emptied or to be driven away.

At first, we wonder why the compound was named Camp Red Ball. We knew the story of the Red Ball Express that existed during World War II when gasoline tankers were expected to follow General George Patten's tank battalions to fill the tanks so they could penetrate further into France and Germany. How did that name apply in Vietnam? The Red Ball drivers continue their mission in Vietnam gassing up tank battalions in the country. They share our barracks. Soon empty tanker trucks are parked in the middle of the field next to our equipment and trucks. The place is soon resembling a parking lot.

Then come the new possessions from the Personal Effects Depot. And guess what? We receive metal coffins for the departed soon stacked 15 high outside the depot's building. The Personal Effects Depot is what you imagine the name conveys…personal effects. Under lock and key, their workers sift through the personal effects of soldiers killed in Vietnam. All belongings are transferred here to be cleaned, sorted and boxed to be sent to soldier's spouses, parents or nearest relatives. This includes stereo systems, radios, clothing, knick knacks purchased locally, and so forth. Photographs pose a uniquely tricky decision-making process because sometimes it is impossible to tell who is the spouse or another lover.

In total, our encampment is becoming a wacky crowded place. Soon arrangements are made to have some vehicles simply parked elsewhere.

THE LEARNING LESSON: Having coffins stacked in your midst conveys death and the war. The absurdity of it is that my daily activities do not reflect our being at war.

PARCELS, DRUNKS AND SEX

Life soon falls into a routine. I travel almost daily to the Saigon harbor to work with ship captains and their crews and stevedores in the mission of offloading large container ships, and getting mail containers transported to our facility.

The men of the 38th BPO are always busy moving the mail, whether opening the containers and postal sacks or resorting all sizes of packages for different unit locations throughout the southern zone that we are responsible for.

At night, men are free to go to our on-site bar where music from a jukebox or an occasional local band blares into the late night, typically until around eleven. This was still relatively early in the war and unlike later in the war, drugs were essentially non-existent. The drug of choice is alcohol and does it ever flow. Putting it gently, some of our troops are constantly living in an alcohol fog and it is truly miraculous that we have not had accidents delivering our packages throughout the war zone.

In addition, there is the ever-present desire of many for sex which is as convenient as walking outside the perimeter of our compound to find brothels catering to our boys. I continue the not so fun job of going out before midnight with a good-sized enlisted man to intervene in various sexual trysts. Sometimes, I have to yank fellows out bed. Often, this is immediately followed by a bit of pushing and shoving and that's why I always take "big" guys with me on these "missions". If you saw the condition of these places, you would need to wonder how anyone in their right minds would risk disease by being with these neighborly gals.

And so the months began to pass; thankfully, with no harm to any of us.

THE LESSON LEARNED: Crazy as it seems, one can acclimate to bizarre circumstances, largely unimagined months earlier.

CONGRESSIONALS AND RETRIBUTION

During the really tough months of winter in Kansas while the 38th BPO was in its formative stages undergoing training under brutal winter conditions, you may recall my mentioning that two soldiers took it upon themselves to complain to their Congressman about Major Stinger and his torturous leadership.

When letters from the Congressman came to the Major, he called for a formation and went berserk with vocabulary one would not hear from drunken sailors. The two soldiers were threatened with retaliation, but nothing seemed to occur until our unit transferred to the ship taking us to Vietnam without them.

Somehow, the Major had gotten new assignment orders cut for these men upon their arrival in Vietnam. We all thought we would never see them again, but we were all wrong.

It is a number of months later that our two former unit members suddenly show up at Camp Red Ball. Dressed in filthy fatigues with accompanying tank battalion helmets and visors: fully caked in dry mud, they ask if some of their former colleagues would permit them to take a shower in their barracks. Fortunately for them, the Major is off-site and the two men are hustled off to receive the help they seek.

So, what had happened to these men? Apparently, the Major had reassigned them to a tank battalion in unbelievably tough terrain where the men have spent their time fighting the enemy day-after-day.

The men leave their former comrades with thanks, never to be seen again.

THE LESSON LEARNED: In an autocratic structure like the army, put your head down, take orders, and withstand the torment because there are NO reasonable alternatives.

WHEN HOT AND DRY GIVES WAY TO SUPER HUMID AND MONSOONS

Dust and dirt covered everything. Anyone can learn to live with dirt in their shoes, bedding, and possessions, but not one's rifle. A soldier's rifle has to be taken apart and oiled constantly to ensure it will function. M-16s are pretty adoptable weapons, but in jungle conditions, they require maintenance. No soldier would chance their weapon not preforming.

One never stops sweating in these humid 100+ degree days. Indeed, there is lots of laundry. Washing clothes and cleaning the barracks are done by Vietnamese ladies, who slowly move around the compound chattering away in their native tongue. We call them our "momma-sans". The women are usually dressed in something akin to a pantsuit; a blouse and silk pants. Typically, the women are elderly and never look hot; either by way of temperature or looks.

Dust, dirt and grit can be a nuisance. Not so with mud. And so, continuous hot sunny, humid days give way to overcast days. And then, much as one can imagine found Noah…the rains indeed do arrive. Not just rain, sheets-upon-sheets of rain with small breaks when the sun appears, only to be replaced by new bouts of monsoons. Never have I seen rain come down so hard. So hard, at times, one thinks it is either a total fog or whiteout. And think about this, it is not snow, it's driving rain coming down in every direction, even horizontally. At such times, you cannot see 15 feet in front of you.

Then suddenly, the rain stops and the sun peaks through, followed minutes later, by more driving rain.

THE LEARNING LESSON: Weather can always be worse so stop complaining about it.

Monsoons arrive in the form of torrential downpours followed by rainbows and then more rain and mud. Above: Getting our laundry done the old fashioned way to remove mud everywhere!

MONSOONS BRING OUT THE WORST OF CIRCUMSTANCES AND YET, THE BEST IN PEOPLE

In as little as a day with torrential rains, our yard or field is turned into a quagmire, Walking causes my boots to sink over an inch into the muck. Lovely! It is quickly obvious the utilitarian value of combat boots.

Not only does everything get caked in mud, but the rain brings out rats scurrying around looking for shelter, e.g. finding refuge indoors in our facilities and rooms. And not to be outdone…snakes as well.

And so I am to have the scare of a lifetime!

One afternoon, I journey to my room to relieve myself, only to come face-to-face with the deadliest snake on earth, a bamboo viper. We are about 5 feet apart and I call for help. The snake is probably about 6 feet long.

In comes my Momma-san. She is this little, very old toothless, nettle-nut chewing lady. I would guess her age at about 75.

Holy cow, does she ever move quickly. She grabs a nearby shovel and a broom and as quickly as you can say, "Jackie Robinson", she cleanly slices the head off the snake. Yikes!

Momma-San smiles sheepishly at me, as if to apologize for her country having such critters, and then she calmly picks it up, exits to the outdoors, From the doorway of my residence, I watch as she throws the snake's long body, like a lasso whipping it over her head, some 30-40 feet away into a type of hedge grove. Without as much as saying a word, she then departs for a neighboring building.

Wow! She doesn't show the slightest expectation of a "thank you" from me.

THE LEARNING LESSON: Heroines can come in quite unexpected forms.

HAPPINESS COMES IN SMALL PACKAGES

Happiness comes in small ways and can be interpreted in a few ways:

The first "small way" is mail call. This includes getting letters from family and loved ones, but perhaps more, are the packages from home. This is what my job and my unit, the 38th BPO, is all about...giving soldiers in terrible places far from home, the gift of parcels from home. I cannot describe how these packages are welcomed and prized. They often are valued more than money. In fact, they are sometimes exchanged or bartered for other valued items...gum, cigarettes, tobacco, candy, dry sox,shake 'em puddings, salamis...the list of items is almost endless. These are the days, however, before huge drug use comes to this war zone. Packaged bombs from the home front are also not yet a reality.

The second most valued way soldiers in the field draw happiness is from having the ability to purchase items that either remind them of home, or serve to simply give them a small amount of pleasure in their difficult existence. This is where a field PX (a Personal Exchange) comes into the picture. Certainly, there are big PX's the size/makeup of large grocery stores or Sam's Clubs in large posts, but when you are out in the "boonies" not so.

Here I am, miles (kilometers) away from the nearest military facility (Tan Son Nhat Airbase), which is north of Saigon. Shortly after getting there, it occurs to me that we need a PX in our compound. In a matter of days, my unit builds a facility to house our own PX. In truth, it is little more than a bodega with a reception-check out table behind which are shelves for items to be sold. My new mission is to buy supplies and manage the facility. This is not to be a "for profit" enterprise, rather a service to our soldiers. I am advanced money to purchase supplies and with a driver learn where and how to buy them in Saigon. I make weekly trips to replenish supplies.

For the remaining time I am here, this store is open a few hours daily to sell all manner of goods...toothpaste, gum, etc.

THE LEARNING LESSON: Helping others has it's rewards; it also provides the opportunity to get away and buy the stuff you want.

FATALISM PERSONIFIED

Fatalism, for those unfamiliar with the term is defined as "the doctrine that all events are subject to fate". Fate, in turn, has several definitions, each somewhat associated with the other: 1. the ultimate power by which the order of things is prescribed. 2. something supposed to be caused by such power. 3. a prophetic declaration of what must be. 4. death or ruin. 5. FATES as in mythology, i.e. the three goddesses of fortune".

So why bring this up? Because one never knows what will be. This is precisely why individuals in combat zones become fatalistic. A person does not fold up into a ball with worry wondering if and/or when they might get killed or wounded. They simply plow on with life one day at a time doing his/her job, a way of living others would think is both foolhardy and dangerous under the circumstances. Honestly, what choices does one have?

And so I travel by van into the city on an almost daily basis to work with stevedores unloading ships. I also visit the PX warehouse, walk the streets of the city, and go to the officer's club for a swim or relax with a quick drink on their veranda overlooking the streets below. I visit a tailor, get a haircut or on occasional, have a massage to release the tension that builds over time.

On the rare occasion of a day off, with camera in hand, I spend a short few hours sightseeing places like Embassy Row, the Presidential Palace, and my favorite place on Sundays…the city zoo. This place is truly lovely and a person would never think it a place where war exists. The many animals there appear well treated, the parklike setting is simply beautiful with lovely flowering plants in colorful arrangements. Families picnic on manicured lawns, and vendors sell peanuts, cotton candy, and other treats for children to enjoy. This truly epitomizes the city's label as the "Paris of the East".

THE LEARNING LESSON: I learn, as we humans learn to do, to live with circumstances previously thought to be hellishly dangerous. Call it "versatility", "adaptability", "flexibility", "foolhardy" or even "irrationality", but the fact remains, I learned life requires taking such chances.

Above: Saigon view from Officers' Club. Below right: Botanical Gardens

and below in front of City Hall.
Presidential Palace and Parliament.

Saigon: "Paris of the East".
From beauty to squalor. Parks,
peddlers, embassies, and traffic
everywhere.

A JOURNEY TO CAM RAHN BAY

I have always been a person who enjoys travel…not to say that some of the journeys described above would be called enjoyable. Nevertheless, there are a few opportunities to travel further afield from the daily trips taken to carry out my mission.

On one occasion, I am asked to fly up to Cam Rahn Bay, the location of our sister BPO that was assigned the mission of handling parcel post for the northern military region of our armed forces (our unit handles the southern region). My mission is to observe their operation, contrast it to ours and discover procedures or processes that could be replicated.

This trip affords me the opportunity to fly in a cargo carrier to another area of the country. I am thrilled to be going, if only for two days. As usual, we drive to Tan Son Nhat Air Base. From there I fly on a C-9 cargo plane to my destination. To my amazement, I discover what had to be, one of the most beautiful beaches in the world. The ribbon of beachfront went on for miles, the sand was simply clean and a brilliant portrait of white. The water is a gorgeous aqua blue. Not what I expected.

Ships are anchored near the postal facility. The buildings are strikingly similar to ours. So are the setup and the operations. The barracks are of wood like our, but no need for mosquito netting over their beds nightly as we do…no mosquitoes here. My fellow officers are friendly hosts and quite hospitable wanting to learn about us and our experiences. They have never been attacked and the war seems more remote to them at their post then is true for my encampment. This is not to say that their vehicles have not faced enemy areas, for they do, because they bring parcels to units constantly under barrage (far more than is true for us in the southern zone).

I learn their unit came to Vietnam after we arrived. They are fascinated by our experiences. They were transported directly by plane from California where they had formed in nice weather conditions in contrast to what we had experienced in the wilds of a frigid Kansas winter.

THE LESSON LEARNED: Vietnam presents many different worlds.

A trip to Cam Rahn Bay. Note the very
different terrain from the Saigon area.

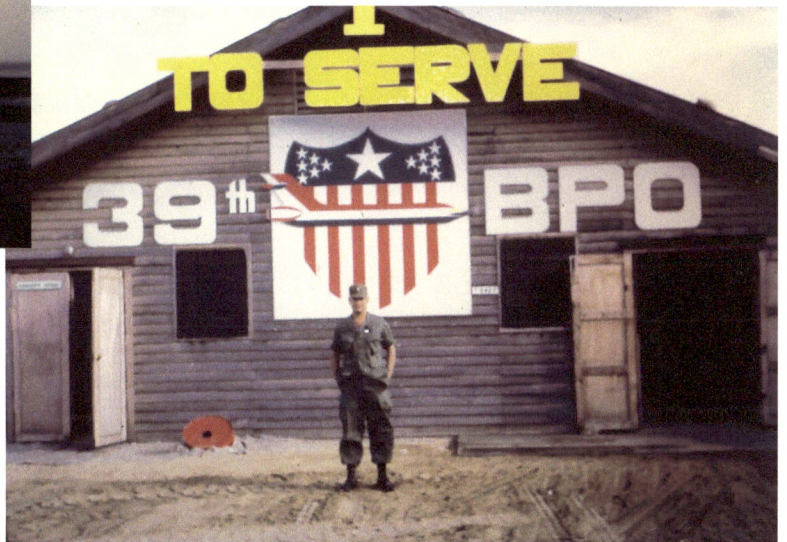

THE JOURNEY FOR A PRIVATE'S DREAM: TO LONG BINH

One day, my commanding officer asks me to go on a unique mission with him to Long Binh Post. The post functions as the U.S. Army Logistics Center, and Major Command Headquarters for United States Army Republic of Vietnam (USARV). The Post is not far from Biên Hòa Air Base.

Officially, these headquarters are located on the east side of Đồng Nai river, 33 kilometers from Saigon, and a little further from our facilities at Camp Red Ball. We ride together for a bit over two hours in the front cab of a deuce and a half truck with a driver. The road to the base, once through Saigon, moves along pretty quickly on what appears as the first US style highway that I have seen in Vietnam. Lots of truck traffic moves along through flat terrain with ribbons of rice fields along the way.

Upon arrival, we discover an enormous sprawling logistics facility and the largest U.S. Army base in Vietnam. There are in excess of 50.000 personnel assigned to this place, and it seems like there are dozens of Generals' vehicles parked in front of the main building (vehicles having one to three star flags affixed to the front of them).

So, what mission is so important that I have to visit headquarters on this day? It is to request a special dispensation on behalf of a private in my unit. And what, pray tell, is his appeal? It is to build a non-denominational church on Camp Red Ball's open land.

After a few meetings, the church receives official General-level approval. Only one condition is established for the approval: the church will receive no army monies and is to be funded entirely by the requesting private and/or contributions by other private parties. The footprint of the church will be determined by the Army. With all this agreed upon, we return to our daily routines while thinking how interesting it will be to see this church actually become reality.

THE LESSON LEARNED: It is a bad idea to ever stand in the way of a religious zealot determined to build a church or offering to his faith.

A trip to Major Command Headquarters for United States Army Republic of Vietnam (USARV)…Long Binh close to Bien Hoa.

SNIPERS

Dinners are eaten in a large mess hall and that's where you find me most evenings eating with a Warrant Officer, not from my unit. We typically eat quickly, exchange stories and adjourn to write letters home or I head over to open the little PX/ Bodega that I manage for the men in our encampment.

Day-after-day grinds on like this, my riding a van or jeep into Saigon to work with the stevedores, make purchases at the main PX or supply depot, or visit places in the city like the Officers Club or to get a haircut or message (to honestly release the pressures of my current existence…not to have sex). On occasion, my driver and I head over to Tan Son Nhat Airbase to pick up our unit's mail and visit briefly with Lieutenant John Scully, who had been with our unit way back (in what felt like an eternity ago) in Kansas.

After several months of this routine, my dinner partner is a no-show. I think that he is off on a small mission, but it also seems funny that he hasn't said anything about traveling out of the area. And then, to my sudden and total surprise, I am told that he had been killed by a sniper while driving his jeep along a rural road. "Surprise" is the operative word because life had fallen into such a routine that I hadn't contemplated death being all around me, that is until it hits so close to home. My unit has had no casualties, except for a few minor accidents, that are nothing to write home about. And now, out of the blue, there is someone gone who had touched my life, not in a significant way, but still as a colleague who was becoming a friend.

THE LESSON LEARNED: Being young, one often doesn't come across death as an interrupter of one's normal activities, but it is always there as a possibility, waiting in the wings.

TRAVEL AS A DANGEROUS WAY OF LIFE

Traveling into Saigon is always an adventure unto itself. First, there are the narrow dirty, dusty roads for the first several kilometers of travel. These roads are often filled with a few slow moving old junkers or carts pulled by Oxen. And of course, there are the motor bikes scurrying around on to the left and right of a vehicle.

Typically, it is a relatively slow go until one reaches Tan Son Nhat Airport and a nearby hospital complex toward the outskirts of the city. Then one can zip along at a pretty decent speed further into the city.

I hardly ever ride as a truck passenger, despite our unit's need to transport hundreds of cargo containers from the port to our unit in the countryside some 10 kilometers away. Normally, I travel by van.

One day as I was riding in the front passenger seat of a van, our tire rod breaks careening our vehicle onto the front steps of single family home. Fortunately, there is only minor damage to the stairs and to the front of our van. It could have been a true disaster. Nevertheless, picture the scene: there are dozens of Vietnamese children, and squawking adults chattering among themselves as we try to flag down a passing American to get the word to any appropriate units to get the vehicle and us out of here. In the meantime, we hand out money as our offering in pigeon Vietnamese in payment for damages and our carelessness.

And then there is the time, one of only a few times that I know of, where I am a hair's breath away from death while in Vietnam. I am sitting in the passenger's seat of a jeep, as we are driving through a main arterial avenue and over a river canal bridge when suddenly a bullet hits and ricochets off the jeep's front dashboard hissing past me and my driver and then coming off the metal behind us again ricochetting into my passenger side foot well. My driver says nothing..I say nothing, just a gasp from each of us as we continue on toward our home destination. What could one say…only a silent thank you to G-d. And yes, I still have the bullet casing.

THE LESSON LEARNED: Best to live life as a fatalist. Providence plays it's hand in our lives every day.

FROM HELL TO HEAVEN IN ONE FLIGHT

Hard to believe that time passes to the point where I am in Vietnam long enough to deserve my one and only R & R trip for "Rest and Relaxation". To guys in the Vietnam, this means an opportunity for single guys to whore around Thailand for a week and come back with a Tiger Eye Ring. For officers who are married, it translates into six glorious days on the island of Hawaii with their spouses. And so these days finally arrive.

Jan and I meet and have a simply wonderful time on the island. We stay at Royal Princess Hotel in Waikiki Beach. The room is "old looking" and small, but who cares; at last, we are together again, even if for short a time.

We make the most of it, traveling from one end of the island to the other. We visit a pineapple plantation, and the family of another officer I know in Vietnam (whose family decedents emigrated from Japan to Hawaii). They show us around their small flower farm. We drive for hours over rough roads to Hana on the other side of the island (that proves not worth the trip because of a draught that has dried most of the ponds there, as well as the waterfalls along the way). On the trip, we look down upon surfers and spend time at the famous Hawaiian Cultural Village. We dine at the Officers' Club with its spectacular view from the top of the mountain overlooking Waikiki. To summarize, it is a whirlwind montage of sights, sounds, and romantic moments.

Unfortunately, it comes to an end with a long farewell embrace and a somewhat tearful goodbye. It's time to be back on the plane to join my comrades in pursuing our assigned existence, fighting our perceived enemies...the Communists!

THE LESSON LEARNED: Life is an enigma filled with moments that are polar opposites...wonderful and painful events, juxtaposed to one another over short spans of time. Being resilient is an valuable attribute in adjusting to these occurrences as a part of life.

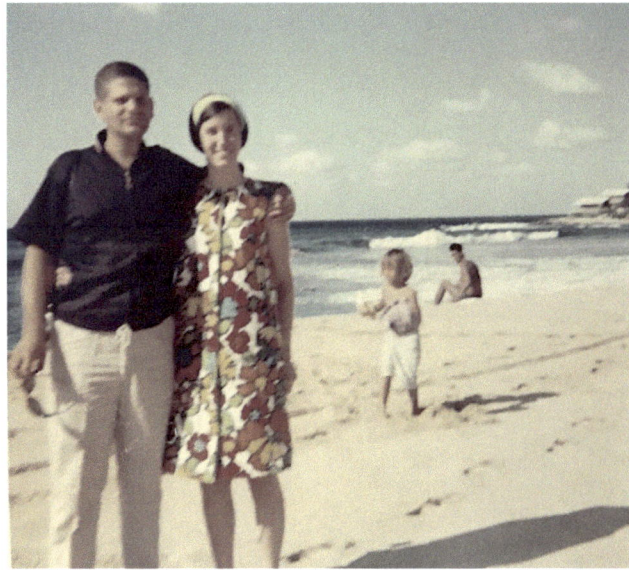

OAHU Hawaii for 7 days of R & R (Rest and Relaxation)

IN HAWAII

NA KUPUNA
NIGHT

BANYAN COURT
MOANA HOTEL
WEDNESDAY NIGHT, 6:

ight in the Gay Nineties
All the fun, songs
m the 'good old days'
and Queen Liliuoka-
buffet.
tax and tip
call 939-811
any Sheraton Hotel

Nº 2860

NA KUPUNA
BUFFET
NOV 1 1967

Date _____

Table No 24

55

"D'ya think it might be catchy, Doc?"

JUNGLE LIFE...HOSPITAL LIFE: PART 1

There are more diseases in this world than one can imagine...some of them are relatively new (AIDS, Ebola, Bird Flu, black mold and new strains of staff infections to name but a few) and only now becoming more well known. And then there are others that we in USA know little about. Ever heard of a Jungle Spore?

I learn about them in infinite detail. They are intestinal parasites that are either one-cell organisms, or as in my case, intestinal worms or a tape worm that lives in the small or large intestine or colon and uses the stool or a person's blood from the intestinal wall as a source of food.

How did I get it? Who knows (it could have been airborne, but more likely through stool-contaminated food or water that was consumed following poor food handling)? It is strange because I never ate locally sold Vietnamese or food consumed on the economy, all for fear of getting sick.

How do I know I have it? Within days, my stool becomes completely watery with white mucus. (Sorry for the description). I do not suffer from stomach cramps. In fact, the urge to go often become a way of life. Soon I feel tired; my skin is pale due to reduced absorption of minerals and vitamins. I begin to lose a huge amount of weight dropping 15 pounds in about 7 days. No one else has these symptoms.

I see a medic and it isn't long before I am hospitalized in the Parasitic Disease Ward. Stool samples are taken. I am given a barium capsule that is swallowed and passes into my stomach and beyond. An injector-like plunger is pushed to extract a portion of my inners for analysis. My clothes are falling off due to weight loss and under other circumstance, I would be thrilled with this outcome...this, however, is not the way to do it! And throughout these days, until a protocol takes hold, I continue losing weight.

THE LESSON LEARNED: One cannot live life with constant worry, but there are many critters out there ready to do us harm (and one found me).

HOSPITAL LIFE: PART 2

Treatment for my Intestinal Parasite begins in earnest with the assurance that it will be successful assuming the source of infection can be eliminated. The surprising treatment is large doses of folic acid.

I take these days of hospital life as a respite from the military life I had been leading. Accommodations are quite reasonable, i.e. a comfortable bed, small talk with others and good food to boot. Of course, there are the occasional eye opening moments when new arrivals enter our ward. One example is of a Colonial who is carried in because he was so emaciated that he can no longer walk on his own. He had identical symptoms to mine except he refused to hearken to what was happening to his body. Within five weeks, he had lost over 60 pounds and was quickly moving to his demise. He is down to 120 pounds, a small version of his former self.

The hospital is open aired having large windows, a large courtyard, white walls and red tiles on the floor. My ward is a relatively quiet place.

The hospital tries to provide some entertainment to break up the long boring days. One evening we all sit on wooden benches and watch the movie, Mary Poppins. On another occasion, I am personally greeted by Ann B. Davis, the actress who famously plays the housekeeper on the Brady Bunch. It isn't Bob Hope, but who cares; the thought and gesture are a wonderful reminder that we count and are remembered despite being so far from home.

Soon I am healthy again, gaining weight and ready to go back to work.

THE LESSON LEARNED: Thank heavens for modern medicine and great hospital care. Probably, in previous wars, I would not have survived.

THE "SHORT-TIMER"

When getting down to about 45 days left to my duty tour, I become more anxious; the name given to such soldiers, is "short-timer". Soldiers start teasing that person about leaving their buddies, the "fabulous food", the warmth during winter, the lovely vegetation of banana trees and nearby rice fields, the scent of spices from native cooking, and the interesting sights and sounds conveyed by traveling through a city like lovely Saigon.

Indeed, Saigon is a fascinating city. It can be both beautiful and like most cities, dangerous. As "Paris of the East", it is a Capital City with cafes in abundance, lovely houses, especially in the wealthier Embassy area, numerous parks, with a parliament and numerous government buildings reflective of Paris architecture; the results the French inhabitants who resided there. Additionally, it has many rivers, a myriad of motorcycles, the constant din of car horns, numerous alleys and street peddlers of every sort. The city brings out extremes, from street panhandlers, peddlers of every sort, to women walking as if on air gorgeously dressed in their long Vietnamese aodai dresses with trailing silk trains.

When traveling in vehicles outside our protected compound, I decide to put on my flack jacket. Although everyone is issued a flack jacket, no one would wear it in that it cannot be worn comfortably in the tropics. But like every "short-timer", I change my thinking on this, as well as my routines. I constantly watch my surroundings. I begin delegating more frequently, assigning more projects to others. Calendar days get marked off one-by-one, but time moves ever more slowly.

And finally, one day when off from work, I decide to put off another enjoyable trip into the city with camera in hand to see the Zoo, as well getting that swim and that drink at the Officers' Club. I even forego a massage, and walking those now familiar streets. I decide it is better to try reading a book, taking a nap, having an afternoon beer and listening to a juke box in the on-site bar and grill. Bottom line: I am not about to take any unnecessary chances.

THE LESSON LEARNED: The quote, "Better safe than sorry" comes to mind as a "short-timer's" most favored jargon.

Traveling into Saigon becomes more frightening and less beautiful when one becomes a "short-timer".

SCARY CALM

As my time counts down, I am awarded a second Army Commendation Medal for the unique service I have rendered for my men, which includes doing my day job, and also setting up our very unique little PX. I feel honored.

The last two to three weeks in Vietnam becomes unusually disconcerting. Word arrives, suggesting there appears to be unusual chatter among Vietnamese which has conveyed a sense that there could be an imminent attack or stepped up Viet Con attacks in general.

Our Vietnamese contacts seem more serious and somewhat distant. Our "momma sans", our forever chattering black teeth, continual beetle nut chewing housekeepers, are falling silent upon our approach. This is especially strange because we cannot understand a word of Vietnamese.

And then, in the distance, not miles away we hear the sound of air sorties dropping bombs and perhaps agent orange with smoke rising in the distance. Scary stuff.

Scarier still are the nights, for here we experience a new occurrence. Before we were pretty much unfazed with the open rice paddies on two sides and the shanty-vile type of buildings on the other two sides just outside our compound. Now we are becoming hyper-sensitive to what exists immediately outside the fencing and sandbags of our compound.

Our men are dissuaded by locals from visiting their establishments; not that the military favors this action in the first place. To put it plainly, we are raising our guard which in this case means literally, increasing our guard. We double the number of guards in our guard towers and our watch shifts are reduced in length to assure vigilance.

THE LESSON LEARNED: Have you had that hunch that something is "off"; that nagging feeling? To say the least, in a combat zone, this is not what you and your comrades want to feel. When the air campaign gets closer, security and watching each other's back become paramount.

Time grinds on slowly… soldiering on: climbing around ships, overseeing sorting of parcels, and watching Pvt. McClung's church getting built.

EERIE SILENCE

During my last two weeks in Vietnam we are no longer having drinks and listening to live music from visiting Vietnamese bands or from the jukebox in the bar/cafe. Instead, we take turns hiding behind sandbags against our exterior fencing and looking across the rice patties to see who is out there. My assignment is to look out toward a neighboring house with its palm trees, beyond the rice patties, some 150 yards away to observe if there is unusual activity out there. We have binoculars but no night vision glasses to judge what is occurring outside our compound.

Are Viet Con really coming our way?

We are many kilometers from Tan Son Nhat, our closest location for reinforcements, amongst the rice fields in the middle of nowhere, so what are we protecting? We have our barracks, thousands of mail pouches and packages for delivery, several Red Ball Express trucks, a few panel trucks and jeeps, a bunch of cargo containers stacked two high (perhaps to 35 feet high) and a bunch of coffins also stacked high to 40 feet, stored here, for the Personal Effects Depot. Oh yes, and our new New England-like church. Bottom line: Not much here worth dying for.

What is to happen next to make our nights more scary still? Something entirely new occurs…flares on parachutes that descend throughout the night from planes that swoop in from somewhere to drop these flares from on high. It is these flares and accompanying orders that create our new existence. Imagine looking out across rice fields with the eerie reflection of flares upon the rice paddy water below. Yes, the amber color of flares slowly descending as they arch back and forth, and the occasional sound of the flare as it gets closer and eventually is snuffed out in water…and nothing more…just silence.

THE LESSON LEARNED: Horror movies don't compare to real life drama in the face of possible combat.

Above: Private McClung's church gets completed and dedicated.
Below: Erie times: Sandbag duty moves forward in earnest.

Staff becomes "shy" and more distant.

Above: Fighter jets fly sorties continually nearby and drop flares above at night. We wear full combat gear for future fire-fights.

Below: Bunker mentality sets in…we get armed to the teeth.

Vietnam (with the VC Tet offensive imminent),
Meanwhile, our neighbors go on with life as usual in their fields. BUT, "life as usual" with the oncoming of the enemy's Tet Offensive proves not to be peaceful for the 38th BPO.

Numerous casualties after the Vietcong overrun the 38th BPO complex... so many incoming mortar and other rounds of gunfire that air evacuation helicopters could not land.

CITATION

BY DIRECTION OF THE SECRETARY OF THE ARMY

THE ARMY COMMENDATION MEDAL
(FIRST OAK LEAF CLUSTER)
IS PRESENTED TO

FIRST LIEUTENANT DONALD C. STRAUSS, 05019200, ADJUTANT GENERAL'S CORPS
UNITED STATES ARMY

FOR THE PERFORMANCE OF EXCEPTIONALLY MERITORIOUS SER-

VICE IN SUPPORT OF THE UNITED STATES OBJECTIVES IN THE

COUNTERINSURGENCY EFFORT IN THE REPUBLIC OF VIETNAM

DURING THE PERIOD

JANUARY 1967 TO JANUARY 1968

THROUGH HIS OUTSTANDING PROFESSIONAL COMPETENCE AND DE-

VOTION TO DUTY HE CONSISTENTLY OBTAINED SUPERIOR RESULTS.

WORKING LONG AND ARDUOUS HOURS, HE SET AN EXAMPLE THAT

INSPIRED HIS ASSOCIATES TO STRIVE FOR MAXIMUM ACHIEVE-

MENT. THE LOYALTY, INITIATIVE AND WILL TO SUCCEED THAT

HE DEMONSTRATED AT ALL TIMES MATERIALLY CONTRIBUTED TO

THE SUCCESSFUL ACCOMPLISHMENT OF THE MISSION OF THIS COM-

MAND. HIS PERFORMANCE WAS IN THE BEST TRADITIONS OF THE

UNITED STATES ARMY AND REFLECTS GREAT CREDIT UPON HIMSELF

AND THE MILITARY SERVICE.

RUN LIKE YOU NEVER HAVE BEFORE!

FINALLY, it is time to leave my unit and head home, not to Jan and Illinois where she resides. No, rather to New Jersey, the address from whence I started my military career. That, of course, assumes that I would get there, a situation becoming more in a question with each passing hour.

Snipers and mortar attacks are becoming more prevalent, although fortunately, that hasn't occurred on my watch or during my daily routine traveling to the docks in the Saigon harbor.

My duffle bag is fully packed and put it in a van. My driver and I depart about 2 a.m. for a return trip to the Ben Hoa air strip, where a flight is to take me home.

Upon arriving at Ben Hoa, I am driven to an enlisted mens' barracks, a building adjacent to the end of a long air strip. I remove my duffle bag from the van and and go into the building. There are dozens of other men waiting with me. We are told to make a line with our belongings from one end to other end through the middle of the building. We can look out toward the runway, but observe nothing but darkness. Suddenly, all the tarmac lights came on and in the distance, we see an approaching commercial aircraft coming in for a landing. The plane slows as it gets to the end of the runway which is some 100 yards away. It finishes taxiing and turns its nose toward the runway.

I can see plainly that it is a commercial Eastern Airlines Plane. A more beautiful sight is not to be seen. The plane's door swings open pushed by a stewardess. Two soldiers run out to push a mobile staircase up to the plane. At that moment, all hell breaks out. One can hear incoming mortar rounds coming in, at first sounding distance, but quickly coming closer toward the plane. Someone in the barracks yells for us to get out of here in single file. As I leave the building with duffle bag over by shoulder, I run for all I am worth. I have never scrambled up a staircase faster in my life. My life and the lives of others behind me, literally, depend on it!

THE LESSON LEARNED: When you fear for your life, you attain physical achievement at heights unimagined beforehand.

PANDEMONIUM

In a matter of seconds, I have sprinted across that tarmac and up those stairs. I am through that aircraft door and suddenly transported into an idyllic new world, much like Dorothy in The Wizard of Oz. A pretty stewardess takes me several steps down the aisle, has me toss my duffle bag into a cabinet above, and has me sit so others can pass. As one of the last to enter the plane, I find myself in the equivalent of First Class, but who cares.

The cabin is filled with fear-filled, wide-eyed frozen faces. Few sounds are heard except for the engines and booms coming from incoming mortar rounds. The words "buckle up" are hardly shouted when the plane's pilot guns the engines and the plane lurches forward and continues accelerating down the tarmac. Moments later, we are airborne. Looking out the window as we make a vertically banked turn, I look down and see the mortar rounds dropping into the zone which seconds before we vacated.

An enormous roar erupts from everyone. Pandemonium erupts! There is hooting and hollering, screaming and scouting, a crescendo of happiness expressed like none I have ever heard. The energy level is sky high. The relief unimaginable.

Beyond that, matters turn quiet again as most everyone soon falls asleep from exhaustion and having been up through the night. The adrenaline rush has passed. We wing our way east to Wake Island in the Pacific Ocean, a tiny island just big enough to hold an airstrip so we can refuel and head back to the good old USA! Not much to the island except a few buildings and an airstrip. Next stop for refueling is Hawaii and then we are back in the USA; home at last, to moments of happiness, but also new trials and tribulations thanks to time in Vietnam.

Once through that plane's entry door, I experienced the closest thing to a time portal shown in sci-fi movies. Within seconds, our plane leaves the misery of war behind. Each foot of rising elevation pushes us toward to a new destination and future lifestyle.

THE LESSON LEARNED: All's well that ends well!

Our destination on the way out!
Island hopping home.

Right before departing from
Army newspaper: lies…lies…lies.

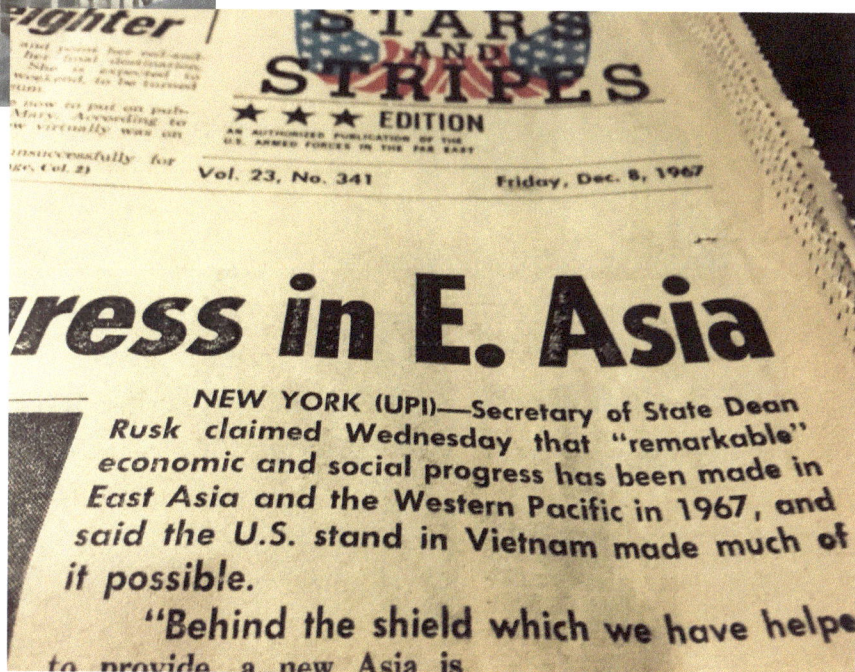

STARS AND STRIPES
★ ★ ★ EDITION

AN AUTHORIZED PUBLICATION OF THE
U.S. ARMED FORCES IN THE FAR EAST

Vol. 23, No. 341   Friday, Dec. 8, 1967

...ress in E. Asia

NEW YORK (UPI)—Secretary of State Dean
Rusk claimed Wednesday that "remarkable"
economic and social progress has been made in
East Asia and the Western Pacific in 1967, and
said the U.S. stand in Vietnam made much of
it possible.

"Behind the shield which we have helpe[d]
to provide a new Asia is

HATRED AT HOME

No need to expound upon the happiness I feel seeing Jan, my parents, my immediate family and friends again. Those are moments of pure joy. They last for only a few days and then life intervenes. Jan and I face the issue of having to relocate from my parents' house as soon as possible and that depends on finding employment. To that end, my resume is fully current and sent out to numerous companies.

I receive my DD 214 and Honorable Discharge from the folks at Fort Dix, New Jersey.

Next stop, the local New Jersey Unemployment Office to collect assistance until a job offer is received. This is where I am greeted with my first surprise. "Sorry", I am told. "Your record shows that you were given two weeks of pay upon departure from the military. You need to wait through these two weeks and two additional weeks before you are eligible for unemployment".

I reply, "Those two weeks pay are in lieu of R & R (Rest and Recreation) since being in Vietnam didn't allow R & R, as I might have gotten had I been assigned to Korea, Germany, or other locations worldwide".

To my comment, the Unemployment Office clerk replies, "Tough luck. You fought in Vietnam; better to have made peace than war. Sorry, you got your R & R money; now wait your turn".

Fortunately, I quickly receive a wonderful offer of employment from Exxon and never collect a dime of unemployment.

THE LESSON LEARNED: Civilians who have never served have no idea how difficult life overseas in the military can be. Life overseas is a lonely, difficult existence despite being with other soldiers (comrades). The Vietnam War brought out the worst hatred and actions on the part of "peaceniks" and others toward innocent soldiers who returned from Vietnam. They were just doing their jobs, not determining that we should have been there in the first place.

BAMBOOZLED...ALL IN THE PURSUIT OF GREED

Having worked for a few months in Franklin Park, New Jersey and rented an apartment nearby in Parsippany, New Jersey, I think it wise to get my teeth cleaned. I don't feel any tooth pain, but it is over a year since my last dentist visit. I choose a dentist near my office so I can easily visit after work. In fact, at age 26, I have never had a cavity or other dental work done, other than cleanings.

The dentist takes some expected X-rays. Then, to my surprise, the dentist announces that he has found 14 cavities that have to be cleaned out and then filled. I am dumbstruck and question his analysis. Clearly, I have no pain. He says I will soon feel the pain and tells me that the water in Vietnam is the cause of my issue after I stupidly tell him that I recently returned from there.

I decide to get a second opinion from the VA. Subsequently, I travel to Newark and have my teeth checked by the Veteran's Administration dentist. He takes more X-rays and concludes that my teeth are perfectly fine. Again, stupidly, I do not go for a third opinion and think the VA just wants to save money, the reason for my teeth getting a clean bill of health. My mother had great teeth, virtually no cavities over the years; my dad had terrible teeth, and had them removed for false teeth. Whose teeth did I inherit?

So what to do? I have my teeth drilled and filled for hundreds of dollars. Jan then finds a dentist near home, a Doctor Fox, who she loves. When my next appointment for cleaning comes around, I go to Doctor Fox. He says, "I don't like the looks of the way some of your teeth were done". He does not push to redo my fillings. I tell him about the other dentist, my visit to the VA and the dilemma that ensued. Doctor Fox is sympathetic and says that he thinks that I made a big mistake going forward and getting my teeth drilled. Apparently, I had found an unscrupulous dentist able to bamboozle a young x-GI from Vietnam.

THE LESSON LEARNED: "Stupid is, what stupid does" is a description of me in the situation above. Over the years, I have had trouble and major expenses based on those initial, unneeded fillings.

UNCLE SAM AGAIN WANTS YOU

Several months pass, and a letter arrives indicating that my obligation to my country is not complete. What? Indeed, the letter states that I have been assigned to a reserve unit that meets in an armory in the Central Ward of Newark. Mind you, the Central Ward is the center of the riots following the assassination of Martin Luther King. The ward has block-after-block of remnants of vacant buildings that had been fire torched.

Standing in the midst of all this is an armory that houses my reserve unit. It is surrounded by fencing, but the parking lot is so small, parking of our vehicles cannot be done there for lack of space.

I report in for duty, and stand in formation much as I did way back in Indian Town Gap, PA. This is followed by the unit breaking up into small groups to "prepare for summer camp". And what is summer camp? It is our unit's obligation to process new inductees into the Army in Fort Dix, New Jersey, much the same as was done in El Paso, Texas. Remember, the Vietnam War continues in 1969 and 1970, much the same as when I was there.

The Lt Colonel is a "gung-ho" X-West Point graduate, who loves playing military leader. He never went to Vietnam, instead assigned couch-type duties. In other words, I find myself with another ex-Vietnam officer reporting to a guy who is totally egocentric and egomaniacal.

He sends soldiers out with live weapons to shoot to kill, if our men encounter civilians, local poor African Americans, attempting to damage or steal our vehicles. According to regulations this is is absolutely "a no-no". Nevertheless, we lose vehicles, hub caps and other car parts during every meeting because cars are parked blocks from the Armory. Within months, our armory is broken into and we lose our weapons to the street.

THE LESSON LEARNED: There are different kinds of wars. There is the big army wars like in WWI, Korea and WWII. And there is the kind of war I lived first hand. It is "asymmetrical war", where enemies live with everyday folks, and attack authorities and others when they perceive that they can get away with it. It was fought by George Washington and again in Vietnam, in Iraq and Afghanistan. Such war is virtually impossible to win.

LUCKY ME;...NOT SO FOR OTHERS

A few months following my return from Vietnam, Jan and I receive an invitation to visit a fellow soldier on Long Island, a soldier who had been in my Vietnam unit. He has just returned from the war and is anxious to share the news of what had transpired subsequent to my departure from Vietnam.

We drive to Long Island and spend only an hour or two visiting. What I learn makes me feel ill. First, no less than about three weeks following my departure, the Viet Con initiated their Tet Offensive military campaign. Second, the campaign resulted in catastrophic damage to my 38th Base Post Office facility and the men in my unit.

As described in his book, *The Tet Offensive: Politics, War, and Public Opinion (Vietnam: America in the War Years),* David Schmitz writes, "On January 30, 1968 approximately 84,000 North Vietnamese Army and National Liberation Front forces launched nearly simultaneous attacks against over 100 cities and military installations in South Vietnam. The well-coordinated urban attacks came during the most sacred of Vietnamese holidays and caught American commanders by surprise. The results of the Tet Offensive were monumental, tens of thousands were killed and many more wounded. But its importance goes far beyond its military outcome to the powerful political, psychological, and economic impact in the United States".

Our compound, Camp Red Ball, was destroyed by the Viet Con using that location's church steeple as the ground zero for launching incoming rockets. Incoming rounds were in such numbers that many in my unit were wounded (none killed). Air evacuation helicopters could not fly in due to constant gunfire. My first sergeant, a WWII and Korean War vet (with only a few months to retire after 29+ years of service) lost a leg and had his stomach blown in by shrapnel. Our radio man almost died. A Lieutenant Gumsrud, who replaced me, had to be air evacuated to Hawaii. Nothing more need be said.

THE LESSON LEARNED: Events occur in mysterious ways. Is it fate? Does it seem at times that circumstances have been predetermined for or against us, i.e. beyond anything we can do to change outcomes?

IT AIN'T OVER YET: SUMMER CAMP AND MY FINAL FAREWELL

Once a month, at the end of a busy work day at Exxon in Florham Park, New Jersey, I am required to change into my uniform and travel to Newark to attend my reserve army unit meetings. Jan and I can't believe the fact that I completed my overseas tour and active military career only to now become a part-time civilian playing Mr. Career Officer. True, I am promoted to the rank of Captain, but I want to get on with my life, settle down, make money, focus on my civilian career, get a house, have kids, etc.

Meanwhile, I spend time in Newark during meetings just chatting with other officers while the sergeants drill the men, and have them work on projects. The First Sergeant is occupied putting together the "morning report" (the attendance logs) for reporting to higher ups. The Lt. Colonel (Mr. Spit and Polish) is focused on summer camp, our two week venture to process more men through the Fort Dix Army Reception Station. For me, it is a job that I did for months at Fort Bliss. For him, however, it is his opportunity to strut around and show his stuff.

And so, our general meetings that start at 6 P.M. and end at 10 P.M. became a new program of meeting for another 1 1/2 hours to 11:30 P.M. In these extra hours, we must listen to the Colonel tell us how to do the work of managing such a Reception Station. Nothing can convince him from not holding us captive month-after-month, listening to his lectures.

In addition, I have to go to Fort Dix for a weekend to prepare for required duties. Jan and I stay in a motel in Princeton, her trying to keep busy, while I spend two days learning about Fort Dix.

After summer camp, Jan has enough of my late planning meetings. She voices her dislike in the plainest of terms, saying, "Enough already"! My reserve duty commitment and army life are over, as is my military career. Eleven years of military service end in a final whimper, with no ceremony, no special thanks, nothing more. Only one paper is given to me: an updated Honorable Discharge DD214 form.

THE LESSON LEARNED: Military life is inexplicable and completely unique and distinct from civilian life. I learned, "never the two shall meet".

IN A WORLD OF BILLIONS OF PEOPLE, RECOGNITION BY ONE

No story would be complete without a final, unusual story based on coincidence. It took place in the mid-1980's, 16-18 years after Vietnam.

It is the end of a long day of work at FMC Corporation in Chicago. I am heading home to Naperville, talking to a colleague as we move toward the bottom of a packed down escalator. It is rush hour, and we are heading down to our commuter train in Union Station.

Suddenly, I hear someone shouting. "Strauss" from above me higher on the escalator. I half pay attention to the shout, when a second call goes out again, "Strauss". Again, I don't respond. Then comes, "You, Don Strauss, I'm calling out to you". Why, I wonder would anyone be calling my name.

At the bottom of the escalator, I step off to wait and see who called my name. Lo and behold, I am surprised by the sight of John Scully, my fellow 38th BPO Lieutenant, last seen in the fall of 1967. In Vietnam, John ran the letter mail unit out of Tan Son Nhut Airbase and I ran the Parcel Post unit of the 38th BPO in the "boonies". He left Vietnam months before I did.

I am stunned. I say, "John, of all places. How did you ever recognize me and from my back of all the crazy things". His retort, "Don, I would have recognized that voice and accent anywhere". After chuckles exchanging business cards on the spot, we agree to get together with spouses.

John lives in Riverside, and he was the Senior Vice President of Human Resources for LaSalle Bank in Chicago. We do meet with our wives. We all exchange stories over drinks and dinner only once in Oak Brook, Illinois. However, we continue exchanging holiday cards, pictures and brief greetings. John continued his career in the military becoming the youngest Brigadier General in the Reserve Army. He did a tour in Iraq and has since retired on a full 30 year pension. Not bad for a fellow Lieutenant in Fort Riley Kansas and the 38th BPO in Vietnam.

THE LESSON LEARNED: "It's a small world after all" and we are travelers through life, moving quickly through time and space, trying to enjoy life as best we can. We have a brief time on earth, so enjoy life while you can.

POSTSCRIPT: JULY 2016

Two weeks ago, John Scully and I met for breakfast after some 20+ years of seeing each other. Upon seeing him, I could only say that the years have truly flown by. He had aged as I had and we enjoyed catching one another up on our lives since the army…John's multiple jobs that eventually lead to his becoming an international bank Human Resource Vice President and a retired Brigadier General. His having four kids and five grandkids. I told him about my experiences before the Tet Offensive in Vietnam, my lousy reserve assignment in Newark and Fort Dix, New Jersey, as well as my 50 plus years as a Human Resource executive. I proudly discussed Jan, my three children and seven grandchildren. John continues coaching executives for an outplacement firm and I presented my recent Co-Directing experience at the RetireRight Center for 5+ years, in addition to my continuing as an adjunct professor for 25 years in teaching graduate school. We hope to meet again.

After meeting with John, I Googled and found the following recognition of the 38th BPO (displayed on the following pages). Much was accomplished by this small unit and I was proud to have added to it's achievements.

Memorial Days and Veterans Days pass as does patriotic July 4 holidays. The years go by and one has to think of all those voluntary soldiers in far away places like Iraq, Afghanistan, Syria, the DMZ in Korea and other "hell holes", there to protect our nation from those who would do us harm. In many ways, it is sad to think there are those who give up time with families and friends and risk their lives to "do service for their country". Sadder still, that so many think freedom is a gift that comes for free. It isn't free… someone is always out there protecting our liberties. So…in conclusion, I hope, Dear Reader, that you will take a moment to appreciate what you have been given by many before me, as well as those currently in uniform protecting our country from those who would cause you and our nation harm.

DEPARTMENT OF THE ARMY
38TH BASE POST OFFICE
APO U.S. Forces 96388

PERFORMANCE OF DUTIES, 3 MAY 1967 TO 10 FEBRUARY 1968

1. The 38th AG Base Post Office arrived in Vietnam on 3 May 1967 after having been activated and prepared for overseas movement at Ft Riley, Kansas. The unit was activated on 16 November 1966 and departed Ft Riley on 10 April 1967 for surface movement to Vietnam.

2. Upon arrival or the unit in Vietnam on 3 May 1967, it was assigned two primary missions by Headquarters, USARV: a. To provide for the receipt, separation, distribution, routing and dispatch of all surface mail for the III & IV Corps Tactical Zones; b. To provide for the operation of the Army Area Postal Directory for Vietnam. It was given secondary missions of being the Mail Bag and Lock Depository for the III & IV CTZ and maintaining the postal prepacks (equipment needed to open and operate APO's within Vietnam) for Headquarters, USARV.

3. Upon assuming the mission of operating the Area Postal Directory, it was found that there was an extremely large amount of mail on hand (over 100,000 pieces) which had not been properly directorised. There was little or no written operational procedure to cover the handling and directorizing of mail. Through many long, arduous hours, over a two-month period, detailed SOP's were written for each section covering all aspects of operation and the level or mail on hand was reduced to an average level or 65,000 pieces on hand. In addition to this improvement, a much larger percentage of locator mail was being serviced with a good address which resulted in less mail being returned to the sender. Constant improvement in the procedures have continued, with a recorded improvement each month in the amount of mail being received, worked and processed. With the continuous buildup of troop strength in Vietnam the Area Postal Directory has continued to give better service each month with no increase in working space and very little increase in manpower. For the period 1 June 1967 through 31 January 1968, there have been more than 2,100,000 pieces of mail received for directory service. This averaged approximately 8,500 pieces of mail each day during that period. During the same time

1,979,347 pieces of mail were dispatched and 6,387,670 directory actions were performed by the Army Area Postal Directory. At the present there are in excess of 750,000 locator cards on file at this facility. This exceptionally heavy workload has been completed by an average strength of 70 men. Included in the operation of the Area Postal Directory are the essential submissions of processing the hospital mail for all Armv personnel within Vietnam and the operation of the Personal Mail Section which involves directorizing the mail for personnel in transit to the United states Army, Vietnam. These are both extremely sensitive areas and throughout the entire period exceptional performance of service was given in these Areas by members of the Area Postal Directory.

4. The assumption by the 38th Base Post Office of the mission of processing surface mail for the III & IV CTZ took place on 15 June 1967. The objective sought by the 38th Base Post Office on this mission was to move the mail as fast as possible to the 42 serviced APO's. To accomplish this required many hours of coordination with the Transportation Port Command and Movements Control Center of the Saigon Support Command to insure that, upon docking of vessels carrying mail, the mail was unloaded first and that sufficient transportation was available for movement or delivery of the mail conexes. Through constant revision of the requirements and procedures the 38th AG Base Post Office accomplished the mission of offloading mail from the vessels (average load, 80 to 100 conexes) and delivery of that mail to its destination, to the Saigon Air Mail Terminal, or to the 8th Aerial Port for onward movement in less than 24 hours. Such an accomplishment is particularly noteworthy since most of the unloading of vessels and shipment of mail is done at night. This required personnel of the unit to perform their normal duties of processing mail received from units in the III & IV CTZ for shipment back to CONUS and then ride as "shotgun" on mail convoys all night. Although such long hours were often necessary, personnel never complained about these missions but readily volunteered for them. All personnel knew the important morale role that mail plays with the units within Vietnam and contributed without hesitation to its expeditious movement. Movement of mail by motor convoy involved travel throughout the greater Saigon area and within a 20-mile radius of Saigon. Since most of this travel was performed at night, it made personnel of the unit susceptible to possible Viet Cong terrorist actions each time that a convoy was sent out.

5. During the period 1 June 1967 through 31 January 1968 a totel of 6,564 tons of incoming and outgoing mail has been processed by the 38th AG Base Post Office with a monthly average of 635 tons of incoming and 191 tons of outgoing mail. The processing and movement of such a volume of mail, by an average strength of 70 personnel, reflects outstanding devotion to duty and extraordinary stamina.

6. Upon the annual Christmas visit of the Chief of Staff of the Army to Vietnam in December 1967, the 38th AG Base Post Office was called upon to assist in the receipt and dispatch of last minute mail for servicemen in Vietnam from their families in the immediate Washington, D. C. area mail, which was brought by the Chief of Staff to Vietnam. Through the efforts of the men at the 38th AG Base Post Office, this mail was received at Ten Son Nhut Air Base, Saigon, and within 1 hour was on various means of transportation to final destinations. Again, the unit had demonstrated the 'Can Do" attitude which they had shown so often before in their assignment in Vietnam. The last vessel carrying Christmas mail arrived late on the afternoon of 23 December. By the afternoon of 24 December all 110 conexes of mail had been picked up from dockside and delivered to their final destinations or turned over to the 8th Aerial Port for immediate delivery to the appropriate APO. Such an effort required extremely fine coordination between the BPO and the serviced APO's and through the efforts of the personnel of the 38th AG Base Post Office the mail was delivered to the troops located within the III & IV CTZ by Christmas Day.

7. From 31 January 1968 through 10 February 1968 the entire 38th AG Base Post Office demonstrated that the unit was not only a Postal Unit but could also perform the basic mission of every unit in the United States Army, that of meeting the enemy in combat. During this period the 38th AG Base Post Office became an important part of the defense of both Camp Red Ball, a small compound located on the northeast corner of Tan Son Nhut Air Base, and the MACV-Annex located to the east of Tan Son Nhut. The portion of the unit located at Camp Red Ball assisted in repelling attacks upon that installation by Viet Cong forces and during the period 31 January 1968 through 6 February 1968 came under hostile enemy small arms, mortar, and artillery fire, suffering eight (8) casualties, and receiving heavy damage to that portion of the perimeter which they were de- fending. Personnel of the Army Area Postal Directory, who are located at the MACV-

Annex, were called on during this same period to assist in the de- fense of that compound, which was in contact with enemy forces, and also to furnish a task force of 2 officer and 22 enlisted men to assist in the defense of BOQ # 3, located in the vicinity of the 3rd Field Hospital. This facility came under heavy enemy attack and the task force was exposed to sniper fire from streets and alley ways located in the area. It is highly noteworthy that the unit on 7, 8, and 9 February 1968, even though in danger of attack or ambush, delivered mail from the Camp Red Ball area to the Newport dock facilities for loading onto a vessel for shipment to CONUS. Areas through which this mail had to be moved were still under attack at various times by the Viet Cong and, even though such danger existed, the personnel of the unit knew that the mail must be moved and did not let these dangers stop them.

8. The unit has been constantly active in the Civic Actions program since its arrival in Vietnam, assisting orphanages in building, renovating of buildings, conducting English classes, and furnishing materials, much of which were donated by the men of the unit for use by such institutions. They have also undertaken projects to work with Vietnamese units in the immediate area to assist in the development of housing, wells, building of schools, and any other needed projects which meet the objective of the United States Army Civic Actions program. Such actions have led to many friendships with local Vietnamese in the area and have established strong ties between the Base Post Office and those units and institutions with which they work.

9. The 38th AG Base Post office has demonstrated throughout its tour in Vietnam that it has strived consistently to accomplish its assigned missions to a degree above and beyond that normally expected. The importance of getting the mail to the troops in the fastest manner has always been the prime concern of the men. In all situations the unit has shown the "Can Do" attitude regardless of the hardships or inconveniences which were incurred. 'Immediate service' has become an unofficial motto of the unit. Although the 38th AG Base Post Office has been on the active Army roles for just a little over one year, in this short period of time it has demonstrated exceptional performance of duties and has greatly assisted in meeting the objectives of the United States Army in Vietnam. Such

performance has brought great credit upon the unit, the United States Army Support Command, Saigon, and the United States Army.

SAMUEL H. LANGLEY
CPT, AGC
Commanding

www.ingramcontent.com/pod-product-compliance
Lightning Source LLC
Chambersburg PA
CBHW042005080426
42733CB00003B/15